Eight
Fingerless Gloves
to Knit

by

Janis Frank

Table of Contents

Welcome to my latest collection of charming and practical fingerless glove designs, all knit flat on two straight needles. This book gathers some of my favourite previously written patterns, offering a range of projects from beginner to intermediate skill levels. Whether you're just picking up your needles or have been knitting for years, there's something here to inspire you.

Each pattern in this book is designed to keep your hands cozy while leaving your fingers free, perfect for those crisp days when you need a little extra warmth without sacrificing dexterity. From whimsical animals to elegant leaves and intricate decorative motifs, these patterns allow you to create unique, eye-catching accessories. And since all the gloves are knit flat, they're accessible to knitters who prefer working with straight needles.

The patterns offer a balance of simple stitches and engaging designs, allowing knitters to build confidence while learning new techniques. I've included clear, easy-to-follow instructions, and each pattern comes with supporting photos and videos, so you'll never feel stuck or unsure about the next step. Whether you're knitting your first pair of fingerless gloves or looking to add some new skills to your repertoire, you'll find these projects both fun and rewarding.

I've always believed knitting is a journey of learning and creativity, and these patterns are designed to reflect that. I hope that as you work your way through this book, you'll feel not only proud of what you've made but excited to share your creations with others. Happy knitting, and I can't wait to see how you bring these designs to life!

Sizing

To help with the hand sizing, I've included a handy infographic (pun intended). Keep in mind, The gloves will stretch a bit as the stitches relax.

*** Please NOTE! ***

For the fingerless mitt patterns with a decorative motif on the back of the hand, I adjust the needle size to change the fit. This makes designing much easier and ensures the motif, like an owl, spider, hippo, and the like stays perfectly proportioned across all sizes. Plus, it just looks better overall.

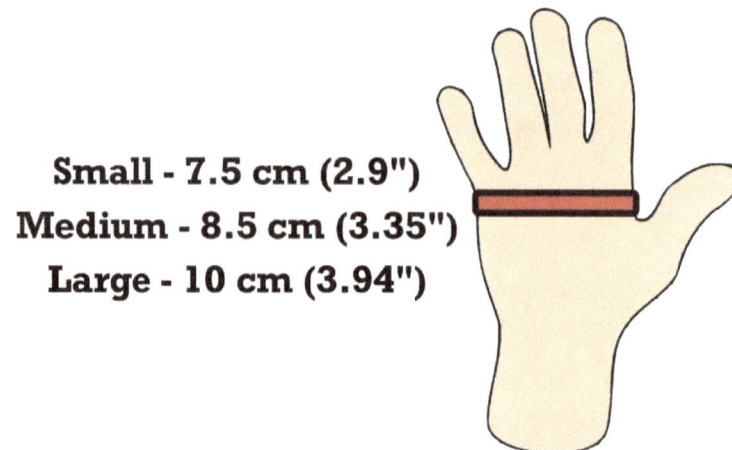

Small - 7.5 cm (2.9")
Medium - 8.5 cm (3.35")
Large - 10 cm (3.94")

Be sure to check the *Abbreviations* section specific to each pattern before you begin. I strive to keep my patterns consistent, but you may notice some differences between them. This is because a few of the patterns in this collection were written years ago, and over time, my writing style and technique abbreviations evolved.

Basic Fingerless Gloves
Knit Flat with 2 Needles

For this version of my fingerless gloves, I'm doing something different. Instead of starting at the cuff, I'm starting at the fingers and working down to the cuff. The reason is because I'm starting to design gloves with 3D animals, characters, figures, designs, etc. Sometimes these figures can only be made from the bottom up. To make it face the right way, the gloves have to be made, how I think of it, as upside down. I needed to design a basic fingerless glove pattern. Because most of the figures are done with stockinette stitches, I wanted the figures to stand out even more. So, I designed the glove to be done with a garter stitch to contrast with the stockinette.

Whew! That was a lot of extra info you probably didn't want. But now that you know the plan, you can check out my website at KweenBee.com to see when I publish new gloves. Fingerless gloves are some of my favourite things to make, so there will ALWAYS be more coming.

Anyways, the pattern is written separately for both the right and left hand. The seam runs along the outside of the hand and along the pinky finger. The thumb is knitted once the hand is completed with picked up stitches. I've included links to videos that will help with knitting the thumb.
This isn't an overly complicated pattern. In fact it only uses very basic stitches and is great if you are

looking for something that is quick to make. Or, if you're a new knitter, looking for something slightly more challenging. As long as you know how to knit, purl and knit 2 stitches together, you'll be able to make these.

Things You Need

And because this pattern is so basic with no pattern of any sort, it's a great knitting pattern to highlight the colour of your yarn. I have a weakness for variegated/shaded yarns. Don't ask me why... My grandma did too. It must be genetic. I took great delight in making the cuffs at the fingers, wrist and thumb in a complimentary shade but you don't have to.

Worsted weight yarn – 1 standard ball of yarn (215 yards/197 m). Any colours of your choosing.

Size 4 mm (size 6 US) knitting needles (or whatever you require to get the correct gauge).

Tapestry needle - to sew the seam and work in the ends.

Gauge

In *garter* stitch

20 rows = 5 cm or 2.5 inches
9 sts = 5 cm or 2.5 inches

RIGHT Hand

Cast on 31 (34, 37, 40)

Row 1: (P1 K2). Repeat to the last st. P1.

Row 2: (K1 P2) Repeat to the last st. K1.

Repeat these 2 rows for a total of 6 rows.

If you want to switch colours, do so now.

Row 7 – 12: Knit across

Row 13: K12 (14, 16, 18) Cast on 13 (13, 15, 15) sts. K19 (20, 21, 22). Total of 44 (47, 52, 55) sts.

Row 14 – 16: Knit across

Row 17: K12 (14, 16, 18) K2tog K9 (9, 11, 11) K2tog K19 (20, 21, 22). Total of 42 (45, 50, 53) sts

Row 18 – 20: Knit across

Row 21: K12 (14, 16, 18) K2tog K7 (7, 9, 9) K2tog K19 (20, 21, 22). Total of 40 (43, 48, 51) sts

Row 22 – 24: Knit across

Row 25: K12 (14, 16, 18) K2tog K5 (5, 7, 7) K2tog K19 (20, 21, 22). Total of 38 (41, 46, 49) sts

Row 26 – 28: Knit across

Row 29: K12 (14, 16, 18) K2tog K3 (3, 5, 5) K2tog K19 (20, 21, 22). Total of 36 (39, 44, 47) sts

Row 30 – 32: Knit across

Row 33: K12 (14, 16, 18) K2tog K1 (1, 3, 3) K2tog K19 (20, 21, 22). Total of 34 (37, 42, 45) sts

Stop here for **SMALL** and **MEDIUM** sizes. Skip ahead to the row marked with ♥

Row 34 – 36: Knit across

For the LARGE and X-LARGE

Next row: K0 (0, 16, 18) K2tog K0 (0, 1, 1,) K2tog K0 (0, 21, 22). Total of 34 (37, 40, 43) sts)

♥ **Next 13 rows**: K across

If you want to switch colours, do so now.

With the **RIGHT** side facing

Next row: (P1 K2). Repeat to the last st. P1.

Next row: (K1 P2) Repeat to the last st. K1.

Repeat for a total of 10 rows.

Cast off. Be sure to follow the P1 K2 pattern to create a nice, finished edge.

Make the Thumb

With the **RIGHT** side facing, Pick up 13 (13, 16, 16) sts from the additional sts you cast on in Row 13. Pick up the st in the twist formed from casting on. If you need help you can scan the following QR code or click this link – Pick up Thumb Stitches.

With the **WRONG** side facing

Row 1: (K1 P2) Repeat to the last st. K1.

Row 2: (P1 K2) Repeat to the last st. P1.

Row 3: Repeat row 1

Cast off following maintaining the P1 K2 pattern.

Sew the seams on the thumb and side of the glove.

LEFT Hand

Cast on 31 (34, 37, 40)

Row 1: (P1 K2). Repeat to the last st. P1.

Row 2: (K1 P2) Repeat to the last st. K1.

Repeat these 2 rows for a total of 6 rows.

If you want to switch colours, do so now.

Row 7 – 12: Knit across

Row 13: K19 (20, 21, 22) Cast on 13 (13, 15, 15) sts. K12 (14, 16, 18). Total of 44 (47, 52, 55) sts

Row 14 – 16: Knit across

Row 17: K19 (20, 21, 22) K2tog K9 (9, 11, 11) K2tog K12 (14, 16, 18). Total of 42 (45, 50, 53) sts

Row 18 – 20: Knit across

Row 21: K19 (20, 21, 22) K2tog K7 (7, 9, 9) K2tog K12 (14, 16, 18). Total of 40 (43, 48, 51) sts

Row 22 – 24: Knit across

Row 25: K19 (20, 21, 22) K2tog K5 (5, 7, 7) K2tog K12 (14, 16, 18). Total of 38 (41, 46, 49) sts

Row 26 – 28: Knit across

Row 29: K19 (20, 21, 22) K2tog K3 (3, 5, 5) K2tog K12 (14, 16, 18). Total of 36 (39, 44, 47) sts

Row 30 – 32: Knit across

Row 33: K19 (20, 21, 22) K2tog K1 (1, 3, 3) K2tog K12 (14, 16, 18). Total of 34 (37, 42, 45) sts

Stop here for **SMALL** and **MEDIUM** sizes. Skip ahead to the row marked with ♥

Row 34 – 36: Knit across

For the LARGE and X-LARGE

Next row: K0 (0, 21, 22) K2tog K0 (0, 1, 1) K2tog K0 (0, 16, 18). Total of 34 (37, 40, 43) sts

♥ Next 13 rows: K across

If you want to switch colours, do so now.

With the **RIGHT** side facing

Next row: (P1 K2). Repeat to the last st. P1.

Next row: (K1 P2) Repeat to the last st. K1.

Repeat for a total of 10 rows.

Cast off. Be sure to follow the P1 K2 pattern to create a nice, finished edge.

Make the Thumb

With the **RIGHT** side facing, Pick up 13 (13, 16, 16) sts from the additional sts you cast on in Row 13. Pick up the st in the twist formed from casting on. If you need help you can scan the following QR code or click this link – Pick up Thumb Stitches.

With the **WRONG** side facing

Row 1: (K1 P2) Repeat to the last st. K1.

Row 2: (P1 K2) Repeat to the last st. P1.

Row 3: Repeat row 1

Cast off following maintaining the P1 K2 pattern.

Sew the seams on the thumb and side of the glove.

Hints and Tips

If you would like a longer glove, make more rows than indicated with the row marked with the ♥ If you are making a longer glove, cast the stitches off loosely to allow for more stretch.

If you want the cuff to be a different colour than the rest of the glove, I've indicated when to switch colours. The cuff on the fingers, wrist and thumb are don with the K1 P2 ribbing sections.

You don't need to add the extra ribbing for the thumb. It is a finished edge so it won't come undone. You may want to do a quick single crochet around to give it a bit of a fancy edging.

Watch the Helpful Video

If you need help with casting on the thumb or picking up the stitches to finish the thumb, you can watch the quick how-to video on YouTube here - Basic Fingerless Gloves - How to Make the Thumb

You can also take a pic of the QR code below. When you take a photo, a link will pop up on your phone or tablet. Tap the link and the video will automatically start to play.

Abbreviations

k - knit

p - purl

k2tog - knit 2 together

st - stitch

sts – stitches

Woodland Whispers
Knitted Owl Fingerless Gloves

These colourful owl fingerless mitts are made to match my very popular **Owl Beanie** and **Owl Scarf**, also knit flat on two needles. You can either click the link above or click the link in the *More Free Knitting Patterns* section if you would like to make either one; or both ;-).

I've made these owl wrist warmers similar to my original knit flat owl half gloves but with this version, they are knit from the fingers to the wrist cuff like in the previous Basic Fingerless Glove pattern. The owls are made from feet to head, matching the aforementioned hat and scarf. There is a slight difference with the appearance of the owls when made from head to feet and I couldn't live with that. Once you see it you can't *not* see it, if you know what I mean.

And since I was doing a redesign, I figured I should make the cuffs match. So I did. I did two versions of the glove. One with a rolled cuff edge (blue and brown) and one without (green). It is clearly marked in the pattern where to stop knitting and cast off depending on the edging you want. And speaking of the final appearance of the granny gloves, there is no reason that these gloves have to match anything. You can also knit them in a single colour. It really is up to you and what look you are after.

To make the thumb gusset blend as much as possible and match on both sides of the thumb, there are different ways to knit and purl the stitches together. It changes whether it is on the left or the right side of the thumb. It is noted how to knit and purl the stitches in the pattern. I've also added links to a helpful how-to video to show you how. You don't have to make the stitches the way I did, but it gives a much better overall look. There's more about this in the *Hints and Tips* section.

If casting on the 13 stitches for the thumb or picking up stitches is confusing for you, there is also a video to help you with that too. The link is after the *Hints and Tips* section.

Things You Need

Worsted weight yarn – 1 standard ball of yarn (215 yards/197 m) will make the gloves in one colour. Any colour combinations of your choosing will work.

Knitting needles:

  Small - Size 3 US (3.25 mm) knitting needles

  Medium - Size 6 US (4 mm) knitting needles

  Large - Size 8 US (5 mm) knitting needles

Cable Needle

Tapestry needle - to sew the seam and work in the ends.

4 - 8 mm flat back cabochons or small buttons. You can also embroider eyes on if you prefer.

Gauge

In *stockinette* stitch

Small

size 3.5 mm (US size 4) knitting needles
11 stitches every 2 inches (5 cm)
16 rows every 2 inches (5 cm)

Medium

size 4 mm (US size 6) knitting needles
10 stitches every 2 inches (5 cm)
14 rows every 2 inches (5 cm)

Large

size 5 mm (US size 8) knitting needles
9 stitches every 2 inches (5 cm)
12 rows every 2 inches (5 cm)

Right Hand

Cast on 34 sts

◊ **Row 1:** K across

Row 2: *K1 P2* Repeat from * to * to the last st. K1 ◊ Repeat from ◊ to ◊ for a total of 6 rows.

*(Change colour at the **START** of row 7 if desired.)*

To save yourself time if you're changing colours, I suggest that you <u>Work in the Ends While Knitting</u>.

or scan the QR code below to learn how.

Row 7 – 11: K across (*Change colour at the **START** of row **11** if desired.*)

Row 12: P5 K1 P8 K1 P19

Row 13: K14 Cast on 13 sts K6 C4B C4F K6

If you are uncertain how to make the C4B or C4F, you can either click the link or use the QR code

below:

Row 14: P5 K1 P2 K4 P2 K1 P32

Row 15: K35 P4 K8

Row 16: P5 K1 P2 K4 P2 K1 P5 P2tog (Slip the next st onto your working needle. Pick up the next st,

twist and place back on your non-working needle. Pass the slipped st back onto the non-working

needle. Purl the sts together from LEFT to RIGHT). P9 P2tog (Purl these sts together from RIGHT to

LEFT – as you normally would). P14

If you need some extra help with making these stitches, you can click this link How to P2tog and K2tog

to Make the Gusset or take a pic of the QR code below:

Row 17: K33 P4 K8

Row 18: P5 K1 P2 K4 P2 K1 P30

Row 19: K14 K2tog (Knit the sts together from LEFT to RIGHT). K7 K2tog (Pick up the next st, twist and place back on your non-working needle. Knit the 2 sts together from RIGHT to LEFT) K8 P4 K8 This is the same video as above but starts at the how to K2tog section.

Row 20: P5 K1 P2 K4 P2 K1 P28

Row 21: K31 P4 K8

Row 22: P5 K1 P2 K4 P2 K1 P5 P2tog (as before – pass the next st over, pick up and twist next st, pass slipped st back. Purl from left to right) P5 P2tog (P right to left) P14.

Row 23: K27 C4B C4F K6

Row 24: P5 K1 P8 K1 P26

Row 25: K14 K2tog (from left to right) K3 K2tog (as before – pick up next st, twist, knit from right to left). K20

Row 26: P5 K1 P8 K1 P24

Row 27: K across

Row 28: P5 K1 P8 K1 P5 P2tog (as before – pass the next st over, pick up and twist next st, pass slipped st back. Purl from left to right) P1 P2tog (P right to left). P14

Row 29: K across

Row 30: P5 K1 P8 K1 P22

Row 31: K14 K3tog (from left to right) K6 C4B C4F K6

Row 32: P5 K1 P8 K1 P20

*(Change colour at the **START** of row 33 if desired.)*

Row 33 – 37: K across. (*Change colour at the START of row 37 if desired.*)

Row 38: K2tog. ♠ P2 K1 ♠ Repeat from ♠ to ♠ to the end of the row.

☺ **Row39:** K across

Row 40: ♦ K1 P2 ♦ Repeat from ♦ to ♦ to the last st. K1 ☺ Repeat from ☺ to ☺ for a total of 10 rows.

Continue with the rest of the pattern if you would like a rolled edge to match the edging of the owl beanie hat. If you don't like the rolled edge, cast off. Leave a longer length of yarn to sew the seam.

◘ **Row 49:** K across

Row 50: P across. ◘ Repeat from ◘ to ◘ for a total of 8 rows.

Cast off. Leave a longer length of yarn to sew the seam.

Thumb

With the RIGHT side of the glove facing you, pick up the 13 sts you cast on in row 13.

Row 1 – 4: K across (*Change colour at the START of row 4 of the thumb if desired.*)

Row 5: ♦ K1 P2 ♦ Repeat from ♦ to ♦ to the last st. K1

Row 6: K across

Row 7: ♦ K1 P2 ♦ Repeat from ♦ to ♦ to the last st. K1

Cast off. Leave a length of yarn to sew the thumb seam.

Left Hand

Cast on 34 sts

◊ **Row 1:** K across

Row 2: *K1 P2* Repeat from * to * to the last st. K1 ◊ Repeat from ◊ to ◊ for a total of 6 rows.

(*Change colour at the* **START** *of row* 7 *if desired.*)

Row 7 – 11: K across (*Change colour at the* **START** *of row* 11 *if desired.*)

Row 12: P19 K1 P8 K1 P5

Row 13: K6 C4B C4F K6 Cast on 13 sts K14

Row 14: P32 K1 P2 K4 P2 K1 P5

Row 15: K8 P4 K35

Row 16: P14 P2tog (Slip the next st onto your working needle. Pick up the next st, twist and place back on your non-working needle. Pass the slipped st back onto the non-working needle. Purl the sts together from LEFT to RIGHT). P9 P2tog (Purl these sts together from RIGHT to LEFT – as you normally would). P5 K1 P2 K4 P2 K1 P5

Row 17: K8 P4 K33

Row 18: P30 K1 P2 K4 P2 K1 P5

Row 19: K8 P4 K8 K2tog (Knit the sts together from LEFT to RIGHT). K7 K2tog (Pick up the next st, twist and place back on your non-working needle. Knit the 2 sts together from RIGHT to LEFT) K14

Row 20: P28 K1 P2 K4 P2 K1 P5

Row 21: K8 P4 K31

Row 22: P14 P2tog (as before – pass the next st over, pick up and twist next st, pass slipped st back. Purl from left to right) P5 P2tog (P right to left) P5 K1 P2 K4 P2 K1 P5

Row 23: K6 C4B C4F K27

Row 24: P26 K1 P8 K1 P5

Row 25: K20 K2tog (from left to right) K3 K2tog (as before – pick up next st, twist, knit from right to left). K14

Row 26: P24 K1 P8 K1 P5

Row 27: K across

Row 28: P14 P2tog (as before – pass the next st over, pick up and twist next st, pass slipped st back. Purl from left to right) P1 P2tog (P right to left). P5 K1 P8 K1 P5

Row 29: K across

Row 30: P22 K1 P8 K1 P5

Row 31: K6 C4B C4F K6 K3tog (from left to right) K14

Row 32: P20 K1 P8 K1 P5

(*Change colour at the **START** of row 33 if desired.*)

Row 33 – 37: K across. (*Change colour at the **START** of row 37 if desired.*)

Row 38: K2tog. ♠ P2 K1 ♠ Repeat from ♠ to ♠ to the end of the row.

☺ **Row39:** K across

Row 40: ♦ K1 P2 ♦ Repeat from ♦ to ♦ to the last st. K1 ☺ Repeat from ☺ to ☺ for a total of 10 rows.

Continue with the rest of the pattern if you would like a rolled edge to match the edging of the owl beanie hat. If you don't like the rolled edge, cast off. Leave a longer length of yarn to sew the seam.

◘ **Row 49:** K across

Row 50: P across. ◘ Repeat from ◘ to ◘ for a total of 8 rows.

Cast off. Leave a longer length of yarn to sew the seam.

Thumb

With the RIGHT side of the glove facing you, pick up the 13 sts you cast on in row 13.

Row 1 – 4: K across (*Change colour at the **START** of row **4 of the thumb** if desired.*)

Row 5: ♦ K1 P2 ♦ Repeat from ♦ to ♦ to the last st. K1

Row 6: K across

Row 7: ♦ K1 P2 ♦ Repeat from ♦ to ♦ to the last st. K1

Cast off. Leave a length of yarn to sew the thumb seam.

Hints and Tips

If you don't P2tog and K2tog as indicated in the pattern, you'll end up with one very defined line on one side of the thumb gusset, and a much less refined edge on the other. I tried many combos to make the side of the gusset match. Making the stitches as indicated in the pattern allow for this.

This photo is what the thumb gusset will look like if you knit and purl the stitches without following the instructions.

You don't need to add the extra garter and ribbing for the thumb. It is a finished edge so it won't come undone. You may want to do a quick single crochet around to give it a bit of a fancy edging.

You can use whatever you like for eyes. Buttons will work. I used 8 mm flat back cabochons. They come in a variety of colours and sizes. I looked for more realistic owl eyes but all I could find were ones for taxidermy and they were too big, and expensive. I also recommend gluing them on as sewing will take a bit of time.

Watch the Helpful Thumb Video

If you need help with casting on the thumb or picking up the stitches to finish the thumb, you can watch the quick how-to video on Youtube here - Basic Fingerless Gloves - How to Make the Thumb

You can also take a pic of the QR code below. When you take a photo, a link will pop up on your phone or tablet. Tap the link and the video will automatically start to play. The video is for a different fingerless glove style, but is a very similar technique.

Abbreviations

K - knit

P - purl

K2tog - knit 2 together

P2tog - purl 2 together

K3tog - knit 3 stitches together

st - stitch

sts – stitches

Side note: I use both versions of the terminology when it comes to cable stitches. I've been corrected that I'm using the wrong one for both occasions so it's a no win for me. What I mean is that C4F is the same technique as C2F. Just like how C2B is the same as C4B. Do you think of it as the just the stitches you're pulling or the number of stitches you're using in total when you do it? It's a personal choice, I guess.

C4F - Pick up the next 2 stitches with your cable needle. Pull the stitches to the FRONT of your work. Knit the next 2 stitches on your non-working needle. Knit the 2 stitches from the cable needle. Watch this video to see how. How to C4F or Cable 4 Forward.

C4B - Pick up the next 2 stitches with your cable needle. Pull the stitches to the BACK of your work. Knit the next 2 stitches on your non-working needle. Knit the 2 stitches from the cable needle. Watch this video to see how. [How to C4B or Cable 4 Back](#)

Zigzag Elegance Knitted Fingerless Gloves

Once again, I'm back to one of my favourite, smaller projects to knit: fingerless gloves! I've designed a number of different ones over the years with some of my most popular being the **Owl Gloves**, **Spider Fingerless Gloves**, **Hippo Gloves** and the **Autumn Leaves Fingerless Gloves**, to name a few, and included in this publication! Like this pattern, they too are knit flat on straight needles. Over the years I've found that most people prefer this to those knit in the round, though I do have those too ☺

Like the other patterns, and to keep the design on the back of the hand centred, I change the size of the needles to make them larger or smaller. There's more about that in the *Gauge* section with a quick reference info graphic to help you with the sizing. These are designed for adult hands,but if you would like them even smaller for children, I recommend using thinner yarn and smaller needles. I can't help with what the final sizing would be, unfortunately. It'll be a guess on your part unless you know how to do the math.

If you need help with any of the techniques used in the pattern, there are links and scannable QR codes in the *Abbreviations* section after the pattern. All connect to videos that will show you exactly how to do it.

Things You Need

Worsted weight yarn – a standard ball of yarn (215 yards/197 m)

Knitting needles – described below in sizing and gauge

Stitch Holder

Tapestry needle to sew the seam and work in the ends

Gauge

In *stockinette* stitch

Small

size 3.5 mm (US size 4) knitting needles
11 stitches every 2 inches (5 cm)
16 rows every 2 inches (5 cm)

Medium

size 4 mm (US size 6) knitting needles
10 stitches every 2 inches (5 cm)
14 rows every 2 inches (5 cm)

Large

size 5 mm (US size 8) knitting needles
9 stitches every 2 inches (5 cm)
12 rows every 2 inches (5 cm)

Right Hand

Cast on 35

♠ **Row 1:** * K2 P1 * repeat from * to * to the last 2 sts. K2

Row 2: * P2 K1 * repeat from * to * to the last 2 sts. P2 ♠ Repeat from ♠ to ♠ for a total of 8 rows.

Row 9: K across

Row 10: P across

♦**Row 11:** K2 [K2tog K2 YO K2 Sl st knit-wise K2tog PSSO K2 YO K2 Sl st knit-wisc. K1 PSSO] K18 (33 sts) The pattern between the [and] make up the pattern up the back of the hand on the **RIGHT** side.

Row 12: P22 YO P6 YO P5 ♦ (35 sts) Repeat from ♦ to ♦ 7 more times (You can repeat these 2 rows as more than 7 times if you want longer gloves.)

Row 27: K2 K2tog K2 YO K2 Sl st knit-wise K2tog PSSO K2 YO K2 Sl st knit-wise. K1 PSSO K3 M1 K1 M1 K14 (35 sts)

Row 28: P24 YO P6 YO P5 (37 sts)

Row 29: K2 K2tog K2 YO K2 Sl st knit-wise K2tog PSSO K2 YO K2 Sl st knit-wise. K1 PSSO K20 (35 sts)

Row 30: P14 PM1 P3 PM1 P7 YO P6 YO P5 (39 sts)

Row 31: K2 K2tog K2 YO K2 Sl st knit-wise K2tog PSSO K2 YO K2 Sl st knit-wise K1 PSSO K22 (37 sts)

Row 32: P26 YO P6 YO P5 (39 sts)

Row 33: K2 K2tog K2 YO K2 Sl st knit-wise K2tog PSSO K2 YO K2 Sl st knit-wise K1 PSSO K3 M1 K5 M1 K14 (39 sts)

Row 34: P28 YO P6 YO P5 (41 sts)

Row 35: K2 K2tog K2 YO K2 Sl st knit-wise K2tog PSSO K2 YO K2 Sl st knit-wise K1 PSSO K24 (39 sts)

Row 36: P14 PM1 P7 PM1 P7 YO P6 YO P5 (43 sts)

Row 37: K2 K2tog K2 YO K2 Sl st knit-wise K2tog PSSO K2 YO K2 Sl st knit-wise K1 PSSO K26 (41 sts)

Row 38: P30 YO P6 YO P5 (43 sts)

Row 39: K2 K2tog K2 YO K2 Sl st knit-wise K2tog PSSO K2 YO K2 Sl st knit-wise K1 PSSO K3 M1 K9 M1 K14 (43 sts)

Row 40: P32 YO P6 YO P5 (45 sts)

Row 41: K2 K2tog K2 YO K2 Sl st knit-wise K2tog PSSO K2 YO K2 Sl st knit-wise K1 PSSO K28 (43 sts)

Row 42: P14 PM1 P11 PM1 P7 YO P6 YO P5 (47 sts)

Row 43: K2 K2tog K2 YO K2 Sl st knit-wise K2tog PSSO K2 YO K2 Sl st knit-wise K1 PSSO K30 (45 sts)

Row 44: P34 YO P6 YO P5 (47 sts)

Row 45: K2 K2tog K2 YO K2 Sl st knit-wise K2tog PSSO K2 YO K2 Sl st knit-wise K1 PSSO K3. Transfer the next 13 sts onto a stitch holder. K14 (32 sts)

Row 46: P21 YO P6 YO P5 (34 sts)

Row 47: K2 K2tog K2 YO K2 Sl st knit-wise K2tog PSSO K2 YO K2 Sl st knit-wise K1 PSSO K17

(32 sts)

Row 48: P21 YO P6 YO P5 (34 sts)

Row 49: K across

Row 50: * K1 P2 * Repeat from * to * to the last st. K1

Row 51: P1 * K2 P1 * Repeat from * to * to the end of the row.

Row 52: as row 50

Row 53: as row 51

Cast off

Making the Thumb

Transfer the the sts on the st holder back to the knitting needle. With the RIGHT side facing:

Row 1: K across

Row 2: Purl across

Row 3: K across

Cast off

Sew seams along the side of the hand and the thumb.

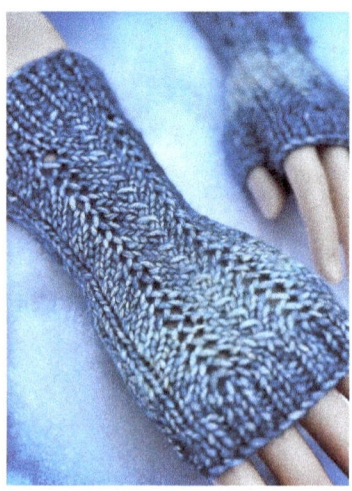

Left Hand

Cast on 35

♠ **Row 1:** * K2 P1 * repeat from * to * to the last 2 sts. K2

Row 2: * P2 K1 * repeat from * to * to the last 2 sts. P2 ♠ Repeat from ♠ to ♠ for a total of 8 rows.

Row 9: K across

Row 10: P across

♦**Row 11:** K18 [K2tog K2 YO K2 Sl st knit-wise K2tog PSSO K2 YO K2 Sl st knit-wise K1 PSSO] K2 (33 sts) The pattern between the [and] make up the pattern up the back of the hand on the **RIGHT** side.

Row 12: P6YO P6 YO P21 ♦ (35 sts) Repeat from ♦ to ♦ 7 more times (You can repeat these 2 rows as more than 7 times if you want longer gloves.)

Row 27: K14 M1 K1 M1 K3 K2tog K2 YO K2 Sl st knit-wise K2tog PSSO K2 YO K2 Sl st knit-wise K1 PSSO K2 (35 sts)

Row 28: P6 YO P6 YO P23 (37 sts)

Row 29: K20 K2tog K2 YO K2 Sl st knit-wise K2tog PSSO K2 YO K2 Sl st knit-wise K1 PSSO K2 (35 sts)

Row 30: P6 YO P6 YO P6 PM1 P3 PM1 P14 (39 sts)

Row 31: K22 K2tog K2 YO K2 Sl st knit-wise K2tog PSSO K2 YO K2 Sl st knit-wise K1 PSSO K2 (37 sts)

Row 32: P6 YO P6 YO P25 (39 sts)

Row 33: K14 M1 K5 M1 K3 K2tog K2 YO K2 Sl st knit-wise K2tog PSSO K2 YO K2 Sl st knit-wise K1 PSSO] K2 (39 sts)

Row 34: P6 YO P6 YO P27 (41 sts)

Row 35: K24 K2tog K2 YO K2 Sl st knit-wise K2tog PSSO K2 YO K2 Sl st knit-wise K1 PSSO K2

(39 sts)

Row 36: P6 YO P6 YO P6 PM1 P7 PM1 P14 (43 sts)

Row 37: K26 K2tog K2 YO K2 Sl st knit-wise K2tog PSSO K2 YO K2 Sl st knit-wise K1 PSSO K2 (41 sts)

Row 38: P6 YO P6 YO P29 (43 sts)

Row 39: K14 M1 K9 M1 K3 K2tog K2 YO K2 Sl st knit-wise K2tog PSSO K2 YO K2 Sl st knit-wise K1 PSSO K2 (43 sts)

Row 40: P6 YO P6 YO P31 (45 sts)

Row 41: K28 K2tog K2 YO K2 Sl st knit-wise K2tog PSSO K2 YO K2 Sl st knit-wise K1 PSSO K2 (43 sts)

Row 42: P6 YO P6 YO P6 PM1 P11 PM1 P14 (47 sts)

Row 43: K30 K2tog K2 YO K2 Sl st knit-wise K2tog PSSO K2 YO K2 Sl st knit-wise K1 PSSO K2 (45 sts)

Row 44: P6 YO P6 YO P33 (47 sts)

Row 45: K14 Transfer the next 13 sts onto a stitch holder. K3 K2tog K2 YO K2 Sl st knit-wise K2tog PSSO K2 YO K2 Sl st knit-wise K1 PSSO K2 (32 sts)

Row 46: P6 YO P6 YO P20 (34 sts)

Row 47: K17 K2tog K2 YO K2 Sl st knit-wise K2tog PSSO K2 YO K2 Sl st knit-wise K1 PSSO K2 (32 sts)

Row 48: P6 YO P6 YO P20 (34 sts)

Row 49: K across

Row 50: * K1 P2 * Repeat from * to * to the last st. K1

Row 51: P1 * K2 P1 * Repeat from * to * to the end of the row.

Row 52: as row 50

Row 53: as row 51

Cast off

Sew seams along the side of the hand and the thumb.

Making the Thumb

Transfer the the sts on the st holder back to the knitting needle. With the RIGHT side facing:

Row 1: K across

Row 2: Purl across

Row 3: K across

Cast off

Abbreviations

K - Knit

P - Purl

st – stitch

sts – stitches

YO – Yarn over. Pull the yarn **FORWARD** under your working needle when **knitting** and knit the next stitch **OR** pull the yarn **BACK** under your working needle for a **purl** and purl the next stitch. Increases one stitch in your work and makes a hole.

YO when KNITTING

YO when PURLING

K2tog – Knit 2 stitches together. Watch the video by scanning the QR code or clicking this link – How to K2tof or knit 2 together

Sl st – slip the stitch onto your working needle. Do NOT knit the stitch.

PSSO – on your working needle, pass the slipped stitch over the stitch just worked. It may be a knit or a K2tog. This and Sl st are a combo that are often done together. Here's the link - How to slip a stitch and pass it over when knitting and below is the QR code

M1 – Make one (knit wise). Increase one stitch between the stitches. Pick up the yarn between the stitches. Twist it slightly and place it on your non-working needle. Knit the stitch. Watch this video on **How to M1 or Make 1** to see how.

PM1 – Make one (purl wise). Increase one stitch between the stitches. Pick up the yarn between the stitches. Twist it slightly and place it on your non-working needle. Purl the stitch. Watch this video on **How to PM1 or Purl Make 1** to see how.

Hints and Tips

If you prefer to knit the last two stitches together on the left side of the design instead of Sl st and PSSO, make sure that you twist the stitch and put it back on your non-working needle. I did this for the autumn leaf gloves I mentioned earlier. You can watch how I do it here - **Motif Edges - Autumn Leaf Half Gloves**

I like using ombre or colour transitioning yarns for these. Solid colours also work well. Lighter colours tend to be better as it can be hard to discern the pattern with dark colours like black, brown, purple and such. Variegated colours would probably make the pattern indistinguishable.

You can make the cuff at the fingers and wrist different colours for a little extra flair.

Make the fingerless mittens as long as you like. I made an additional 7 repeats of the design, but you could do more or less. If you do more you should probably cast on more stitches as the arm get thicker towards the elbow, then decrease down to the number of stitches as written in the instructions.

Easy to Knit
Cable Fingerless Gloves

I'm thrilled to share my latest knitting pattern for fingerless mitts, and yes, my love for these cozy accessories shows no sign of stopping! This time around, I've added a twist—quite literally—with a unique cable pattern that elegantly winds its way down the back of the hand. It's a design element that adds both texture and visual interest, making these mitts a true standout piece.

If you're someone who's mastered the basics and is looking to elevate your knitting game, this pattern is the perfect next step. It's designed to bridge the gap between a beginner and an experienced knitter. And if cabling is new to you, don't worry—this is the ideal project to dive in and learn something new! I've made sure to include video tutorials in the Abbreviations section to guide you through the cabling process, so you'll have all the support you need.

But that's not all! I've also added links to help you with any other potentially tricky parts of the pattern, like increasing for the thumb gusset. I want to ensure you feel confident and supported every step of the way. So, grab your needles, and let's knit something beautiful together!

Things You Need

Worsted weight yarn (less than 100 grams was more than enough to make a pair of large knitted gloves as written. I know because I weighed them). I used Red Heart worsted weight yarn when designing the pattern but any kind will do.

Set of single pointed needles (see note on sizing)

Stitch holder

Cable needle

Tapestry needle to sew the seams and work in ends

Gauge

In *stockinette* stitch

Small

size 3.5 mm (US size 4) single pointed needles
11 stitches every 2 inches (5 cm)
16 rows every 2 inches (5 cm)

Medium

size 4 mm (US size 6) single pointed needles
10 stitches every 2 inches (5 cm)
14 rows every 2 inches (5 cm)

Large

size 5 mm (US size 8) single pointed needles
9 stitches every 2 inches (5 cm)
12 rows every 2 inches (5 cm)

Left Hand

Cast on 36

Row 1: P1 * K2 P2 * repeat from * to * to the last 3 sts. K2 P1

Row 2: K1 ✤ P2 K2 ✤ repeat from ✤ to ✤ to the last 3 sts. P2 K1

Repeat rows 1 and 2 for a total of 6 rows.

Row 7: K15 P1 K16 P1 K3

☆ **Row 8:** P3 K1 P16 K1 P15

❀ **Row 9:** K15 P1 K4 C4F C4B K4 P1 K3

Row 10: Repeat ☆ Row 8

Row 11: K15 P1 C4F K8 C4B P1 K3

Row 12: Repeat ☆ Row 8 ❀ Repeat from ❀ to ❀ 3 times *more.* If you would like longer gloves, make more repeats.

Next row: K12 M1 K M1 K2 P1 K4 C4F C4B K4 P1 K3 (38 sts)

Next row: P3 K1 P16 K1 P17

Next row: K17 P1 C4F K8 C4B P1 K3

Next row: P3 K1 P16 K1 P3 PM1 P PM1 P13 (40 sts)

Next row: K19 P1 K4 C4F C4B K4 P1 K3

Next row: P3 K1 P16 K1 P19

Next row: K14 M1 K M1 K4 P1 C4F K8 C4B P1 K3 (42 sts)

Next row: P3 K1 P16 K1 P21

Next row: K21 P1 K4 C4F C4B K4 P1 K3

Next row: P3 K1 P16 K1 P5 PM1 P PM1 P15 (44 sts)

Next row: K23 P1 C4F K8 C4B P1 K3

Next row: P3 K1 P16 K1 P23

Next row: K16 M1 K M1 K6 P1 K4 C4F C4B K4 P1 K3 (46 sts)

Next row: P3 K1 P16 K1 P25

Next row: K25 P1 C4F K8 C4B P1 K3

Next row: P3 K1 P16 K1 P7 PM1 P PM1 P17 (48 sts)

Next row: K27 P1 K4 C4F C4B K4 P1 K3

Next row: P3 K1 P16 K1 P27

Next row: K12 Pass the next 13 sts onto a stitch holder K2 P1 C4F K8 C4B P1 K3 (35 sts)

❤ **Next row:** P3 K1 P16 K1 P14

Next row: K14 P1 K4 C4F C4B K4 P1 K3

Next row: Repeat row marked with ❤

✪ **Next row:** ♦ P2 K2 ♦ Repeat from ♦ to ♦ to last 3 sts P2 K1

Next row: P1 ☺ K2 P2 ☺ Repeat from ☺ to ☺ to the last 2 sts. K2 ✪ Repeat from ✪ to ✪ one more time.

Cast off

Thumb

Pass the 13 sts on the stitch holder back onto your knitting needle. With the **RIGHT** side facing,

Next row: K across

Next row: P across

Next row: K across

Next row: P across

Cast off

Right Hand

Cast on 36

Row 1: P1 * K2 P2 * repeat from * to * to the last 3 sts. K2 P1

Row 2: K1 ✤ P2 K2 ✤ repeat from ✤ to ✤ to the last 3 sts. P2 K1

Repeat rows 1 and 2 for a total of 6 rows.

Row 7: K3 P1 K16 P1 K15

☆ **Row 8:** P15 K1 P16 K1 P3

❀ **Row 9:** K3 P1 K4 C4F C4B K4 P1 K15

Row 10: Repeat ☆ Row 8

Row 11: K3 P1 C4F K8 C4B P1 K15

Row 12: Repeat ☆ Row 8 ❀ Repeat from ❀ to ❀ 3 times *more.* If you would like longer gloves, make more repeats.

Next row: K3 P1 K4 C4F C4B K4 P1 K2 M1 K M1 K12 (38 sts)

Next row: P17 K1 P16 K1 P3

Next row: K3 P1 C4F K8 C4B P1 K17

Next row: P13 PM1 P PM1 P3 K1 P16 K1 P3 (40 sts)

Next row: K3 P1 K4 C4F C4B K4 P1 K19

Next row: P19 K1 P16 K1 P3

Next row: K3 P1 C4F K8 C4B P1 K4 M1 K M1 K14 (42 sts)

Next row: P21 K1 P16 K1 P3

Next row: K3 P1 K4 C4F C4B K4 P1 K21

Next row: P15 PM1 P PM1 P5 K1 P16 K1 P3 (44 sts)

Next row: K3 P1 C4F K8 C4B P1 K23

Next row: P23 K1 P16 K1 P3

Next row: K3 P1 K4 C4F C4B K4 P1 K6 M1 K M1 K16 (46 sts)

Next row: P25 K1 P16 K1 P3

Next row: K3 P1 C4F K8 C4B P1 K25

Next row: P17 PM1 P PM1 P7 K1 P16 K1 P3 (48 sts)

Next row: K3 P1 K4 C4F C4B K4 P1 K27

Next row: P27 K1 P16 K1 P3

Next row: K3 P1 C4F K8 C4B P1 K2 Pass the next 13 sts onto a stitch holder K12 (35 sts)

❤ **Next row:** P14 K1 P16 K1 P3

Next row: K3 P1 K4 C4F C4B K4 P1 K14

Next row: Repeat row marked with ❤

✪ **Next row:** K ♦ P2 K2 ♦ Repeat from ♦ to ♦ to last 2 sts P2

Next row: ☺ K2 P2 ☺ Repeat from ☺ to ☺ to the last 3 sts. K2 P1 ✪ Repeat from ✪ to ✪ one more time.

Cast off

Thumb

Pass the 13 sts on the stitch holder back onto your knitting needle. With the **RIGHT** side facing,

Next row: K across

Next row: P across

Next row: K across

Next row: P across

Cast off

Sew the seams of the thumbs and along the side of each hand. Work in the ends.

Hints and Tips

You can make the gloves as long or as short as you like. I made 3 repeats of the design. You could do less for a shorter version. The grey pair were repeated 7 times to give you an idea of what it looks like when longer.

Make the seam as narrow as you can when sewing it along the side. Less seam means less irritation. Make sure that it still looks good. If you don't know how, there are a number of videos online that will show you how to do a blanket stitch.

Abbreviations

K – knit

P – Purl

Side note: I use both versions of the terminology when it comes to cable stitches. I've been corrected that I'm using the wrong one for both occasions so it's a no win for me. What I mean is that C4F is the same technique as C2F. Just like how C2B is the same as C4B. Do you think of it as the just the stitches you're pulling or the number of stitches you're using in total when you do it? It's a personal choice, I guess.

C4F - Pick up the next 2 stitches with your cable needle. Pull the stitches to the FRONT of your work. Knit the next 2 stitches on your non-working needle. Knit the 2 stitches from the cable needle. Watch this video to see how. **How to C4F or Cable 4 Forward**.

C4B - Pick up the next 2 stitches with your cable needle. Pull the stitches to the BACK of your work. Knit the next 2 stitches on your non-working needle. Knit the 2 stitches from the cable needle. Watch this video to see how. **How to C4B or Cable 4 Back**

M1 – Make one (knit wise). Increase one stitch between the stitches. Pick up the yarn between the stitches. Twist slightly. Place it on your non-working needle. Knit the stitch. Click this link to watch this video to see how. **How to Make One or M1 – Increase between stitches** or take a pic of the QR code below with your phone or tablet. Tap the link that pops up.

PM1 - Make one (purl wise). Increase one stitch between the stitches. Pick up the yarn between the stitches. Twist it slightly and place it on your non-working needle. Purl the stitch. Watch this video on **How to PM1 or Purl Make 1** to see how.

Autumn Leaf Half Gloves

The inspiration of this pattern came from my *Spider Fingerless Gloves* pattern. I really like incorporating the design into the final wearable piece. I've always liked the leaf pattern and this seemed to be a great way to use it.

There isn't a full-on how to for this pattern, but I have included scannable QR codes to helpful videos to show you how to do certain parts of the pattern. These will certainly help with any of the tricker parts like knitting the wrong side of the YO K1 YO and drawing the edges of the leaves together to a point. To use the QR codes, take a photo with your smart phone or tablet. A link will pop up. Click the link and it will open and automatically play the YouTube video.

Things You Need

Knitting needles:

  Small - Size 3 US (3.25 mm) knitting needles

  Medium - Size 6 US (4 mm) knitting needles

  Large - Size 8 US (5 mm) knitting needles

Worsted weight yarn – any standard size ball will do

Cable Needle - There are a number a styles but I prefer the hook version

Stitch holder – It looks like a big safety pin

Tapestry needle

Gauge

In *stockinette* stitch

Small

size 3.5 mm (US size 4) knitting needles
11 stitches every 2 inches (5 cm)
16 rows every 2 inches (5 cm)

Medium

size 4 mm (US size 6) knitting needles
10 stitches every 2 inches (5 cm)
14 rows every 2 inches (5 cm)

Large

size 5 mm (US size 8) knitting needles
9 stitches every 2 inches (5 cm)
12 rows every 2 inches (5 cm)

Left Hand

Cast on 34

Row 1: (P1 K2) Repeat to last st. P1

Row 2: (K1 P2) Repeat to last st. K1

♥ **Row 3:** (P1 TB) Repeat to last st. P1

Row 4: As row 2 ♥ Repeat from ♥ to ♥ 3 times more. (Counts as rows 5-10).

Row 11: P1 P2tog P21 K3 P7 (33 sts)

Row 12: K7 P3 K23

Row 13: P23 K2 C1F P6

Row 14: K6 P1 K1 P2 K23

Row 15: P23 K2 P1 C1F P5

Row 16: K5 P1 K2 P2 K23

Row 17: P22 C1B K1 P2 YO K1 YO P5 (35 sts)

Scan this code for help
make the YO K YO

Row 18: K5 P3 K2 P1 K1 P1 K22 (35 sts)

Scan this QR code for help with P3.
(The back side of the YO K YO.)

Row 19: P21 C1B P1 K1 P2 (K1 YO) twice K1 P5 (37 sts)

Row 20: K5 P5 K2 P1 K2 P1 K21 (37 sts)

Row 21: P21 K1 P2 K1 P2 K2 YO K1 YO K2 P5 (39 sts)

Row 22: K5 P7 K2 P1 K2 P1 K21 (39 sts)

Row 23: P21 K1 P2 K1 P2 K2tog (When making this stitch, pick up a stitch as if to knit. Twist the stitch and place it back on your non-working needle. Knit the 2 stitches together from right to left.) K3 K2tog (knit the stitches together from left to right.) P5 (37 sts)

Scan this QR code for help with K2tog.

Row 24: K5 P5 K2 P1 K2 P1 K21 (37 sts)

Row 25: P21 K1 P2 K1 P2 K2tog (like you did before: pick up, twist, knit right to left) K1 K2tog (knit left to right) P5 (35 sts)

Row 26: K5 P3 K2 P1 K2 P1 K21 (35 sts)

Row 27: P14 PM1 P1 PM1 P6 YO K1 YO P2 K1 P2 Sl St (as if to knit) K2tog (knit left to right) PSSO P5 (37 sts)

Row 28: K8 P1 K2 P3 K23 (37 sts)

Row 29: P23 (K1 YO) twice. K1 P2 K1 P8 (39 sts)

Row 30: K8 P1 K2 P5 K6 M1 K3 M1 K14 (41 sts)

Row 31: P25 K2 YO K1 YO K2 P2 K1 P8 (43 sts)

Row 32: K8 P1 K2 P7 K25 (43 sts)

Row 33: P14 PM1 P5 PM1 P6 K2tog (pick up, twist, knit right to left) K3 K2tog (knit left to right) P2 C1F P7 (43 sts)

Row 34: K7 P1 K3 P5 K27 (43 sts)

Row 35: P27 K2tog (pick up, twist, knit right to left) K1 K2tog (knit left to right) P3 K1 P7 (41 sts)

Row 36: K7 P1 K3 P3 K6 M1 K7 M1 K14 (43 sts)

Row 37: P29 Sl St (as if to knit) K2tog (knit left to right) PSSO P3 YO K1 YO P7 (43 sts)

Row 38: K7 P3 K33 (43 sts)

Row 39: P14 PM1 P9 PM1 P10 (K1 YO) twice K1 P7 (47 sts)

Row 40: K7 P5 K35 (47 sts)

Row 41: P35 K2 YO K1 YO K2 P7 (49 sts)

Row 42: K7 P7 K10 M1 K11 M1 K14 (51 sts)

Row 43: P37 K2tog (pick up, twist, knit right to left) K3 K2tog (knit left to right) P7 (49 sts)

Row 44: K7 P5 K37 (49 sts)

Row 45: P14 Pass the next 13 sts of the thumb gusset onto a stitch holder. P10 K2tog (pick up, twist, knit right to left) K1 K2tog (knit left to right) P7 (34 sts)

Row 46: K7 P3 K24 (34 sts)

Row 47: P24 Sl St (as if to knit) K2tog (knit left to right) PSSO P7 (32 sts)

Row 48: K across

Row 49: P across

Row 50: K across

Row 51: P2tog (K2 P1) to the end of the row

☺**Row 52:** (K1 P2) Repeat to the last st. K1

Row 53: (P1 TB) Repeat to the last st. P1 ☺ Repeat from ☺ to ☺ once.

Cast off loosely on the **WRONG** side.

Thumb

Pick up the 13 stitches on the stitch holder with the WRONG side facing you. (See hints and tips for more info).

Row 1: Knit across

Row 2: Purl across

Row 3: Knit across

Cast off on the **RIGHT** side.

Sew seam along the side of the glove and the inside of the thumb. Work in ends.

Right Hand

Cast on 34

Row 1: (P1 K2) Repeat to last st. P1

Row 2: (K1 P2) Repeat to last st. K1

♥ **Row 3:** (P1 TB) Repeat to last st. P1

Row 4: As row 2 ♥ Repeat form ♥ to ♥ 3 times more. (Counts as rows 5-10).

Row 11: P7 K3 P21 P2tog P1 (33 sts)

Row 12: K23 P3 K7

Row 13: P6 C1B K2 P23

Row 14: K23 P2 K1 P1 K6

Row 15: P5 C1B P1 K2 P23

Row 16: K23 P2 K2 P1 K5

Row 17: P5 YO K1 YO P2 K1 C1F P22 (35 sts)

*Scan this code for help
make the YO K YO*

Row 18: K22 P1 K1 P1 K2 P3 K5 (35 sts)

*Scan this QR code for help with P3.
(The back side of the YO K YO.)*

Row 19: P5 (K1 YO) twice K1 P2 K1 P1 C1F P21 (37 sts)

Row 20: K21 P1 K2 P1 K2 P5 K5 (37 sts)

Row 21: P5 K2 YO K1 YO K2 P2 K1 P2 K1 P21 (39 sts)

Row 22: K21 P1 K2 P1 K2 P7 K5 (39 sts)

Row 23: P5 K2tog (When making this stitch, pick up a stitch as if to knit. Twist the stitch and place it back on your non-working needle. Knit the 2 stitches together from right to left). K3 K2tog (knit the stitches together from left to right.) P2 K1 P2 K1 P21 (37 sts)

Scan this QR code for help with K2tog.

Row 24: K21 P1 K2 P1 K2 P5 K5 (37 sts)

Row 25: P5 K2tog (pick up, twist, knit right to left) K1 K2tog (knit left to right) P2 K1 P2 K1 P21 (35 sts)

Row 26: K21 P1 K2 P1 K2 P3 K5 (35 sts)

Row 27: P5 Sl St (as if to knit) K2tog (knit left to right) PSSO P2 K1 P2 YO K1 YO P6 PM1 P1 PM1 P14 (37 sts)

Row 28: K23 P3 K2 P1 K8 (37 sts)

Row 29: P8 K1 P2 (K1 YO) twice. K1 P23 (39 sts)

Row 30: K14 M1 K3 M1 K6 P5 K2 P1 K8 (41 sts)

Row 31: P8 K1 P2 K2 YO K1 YO K2 P25 (43 sts)

Row 32: K25 P7 K2 P1 K8 (43 sts)

Row 33: P7 C1B P2 K2tog (pick up, twist, knit right to left) K3 K2tog (knit left to right) P6 PM1 P5 PM1 P14 (43 sts)

Row 34: K27 P5 K3 P1 K7 (43 sts)

Row 35: P7 K1 P3 K2tog (pick up, twist, knit right to left) K1 K2tog (knit left to right) P27 (41 sts)

Row 36: K14 M1 K7 M1 K6 P3 K3 P1 K7 (43 sts)

Row 37: P7 YO K1 YO P3 Sl St (as if to knit) K2tog (knit left to right) PSSO P29 (43 sts)

Row 38: K33 P3 K7 (43 sts)

Row 39: P7 (K1 YO) twice K1 P10 PM1 P9 PM1 P14 (47 sts)

Row 40: K35 P5 K7 (47 sts)

Row 41: P7 K2 YO K1 YO K2 P35 (49 sts)

Row 42: K14 M1 K11 M1 K10 P7 K7 (51 sts)

Row 43: P7 K2tog (pick up, twist, knit right to left) K3 K2tog (knit left to right) P37 (49 sts)

Row 44: K37 P5 K7 (49 sts)

Row 45: P7 K2tog (pick up, twist, knit right to left) K1 K2tog (knit left to right) P10 Pass the next 13 sts of the thumb gusset onto a stitch holder. P14 (34 sts)

Row 46: K24 P3 K7 (34 sts)

Row 47: P7 Sl St (as if to knit) K2tog (knit left to right) PSSO P24 (32 sts)

Row 48: K across

Row 49: P across

Row 50: K across

Row 51: P2tog (K2 P1) to the end of the row

☺ **Row 52:** (K1 P2) Repeat to the last st. K1

Row 53: (P1 TB) Repeat to the last st. P1 ☺ Repeat from ☺ to ☺ once.

Cast off loosely on the **WRONG** side.

Thumb

Pick up the 13 stitches on the stitch holder with the WRONG side facing you. (See hints and tips for more info).

Row 1: Knit across

Row 2: Purl across

Row 3: Knit across

Cast off on the **RIGHT** side.

Sew seam along the side of the glove and the inside of the thumb. Work in ends.

Abbreviations

K – knit

P – purl

YO – yarn over

TB – Pick up the stitch with your stitch holder. Hold the stitch at the back of your work. Knit the next stitch. Knit the next stitch. Knit the stitch from the stitch holder.

Watch how to do the twist back

C1B – Cable 1 back. Pick up next stitch on a cable needle. Pull this stitch to the **BACK** of your work. **Knit** the next stitch. **Purl** the stitch on the cable needle.

Watch how to do C1B

C1F – Cable 1 forward. Pick up the next stitch on a cable needle. Pull this stitch to the **FRONT** of your work. **Purl** the next stitch. **Knit** the stitch on the cable needle.

Watch how to do C1F

M1 – Make one (knit wise). Increase one stitch between the stitches. Pick up the yarn between the stitches. Twist slightly. Place it on your non-working needle. Knit the stitch. Watch this video to see how.

PM1 - Make one (purl wise). Increase one stitch between the purl stitches. Pick up the yarn between the stitches. Place it on your non-working needle. Purl the stitch as you regularly would. Watch this video to see how.

K2tog – How you do this depends where you are in the pattern. If you are making the right side of the leaf, knit right to left. If you are making the left side of the leaf, knit left to right. If you do it this way you eliminate the twisting of the stitch and the edge of the leaf flows evenly.

The k2tog are given for **RIGHT** handed knitters. If you are knitting left to right as a **LEFT** handed knitter, reverse the order that you knit the stitches together. K2tog from left to right then pick up, twist, knit from right to left.

Sl St – slip the stitch

PSSO – pass the slipped stitch over.

Hints and Tips

Make your seams as narrow as possible when sewing them. The bulkier the seam the more noticeable and possibly uncomfortable for the wearer.

Everything between and including the PM1 and M1 stitches form the thumb gusset.

When you are making the thumb, you MUST pick up the stitches from the wrong side. Pass the stitches from the stitch holder to the knitting needle then onto the other knitting needle so the wrong side facing you. If you don't do the second pass, you'll get a weird line.

Leave the cast off end of the finger cuff and the thumb longer so you can use it to sew up the seam along the side of the gloves and seam of the thumb, respectively.

The striped ombre versions of the gloves are done with Loops & Threads "Facets" yarn you can find at Michaels (as of the printing of this pattern). It's thin for a worsted weight yarn and I needed to use a 4.5 mm set of dpn's to get the sizing correct. Make sure to check your gauge and adjust accordingly!

Please be aware that these gloves look like the leaves are off centre when they're not being worn. I actually redesigned them so the motif would be 2 stitches over because when they were on, they looked too close to the thumb. Sometimes designs are weird and the centre of the design visually isn't the middle of the design mathematically or functionally. Ahhh! The joys of art...

Spider
Fingerless Gloves
Knit Flat on 2 Needles

Creepy? No. Awesome? YES! Knit a pair of fingerless gloves with a spider motif on the back of the hand. Guaranteed to never fall off, the 3D spider is created as you make the mitten. This isn't a pattern for beginners.

You'll need to think out of the box a bit for this one; making bobbles and working selectively over given stitches to create the body and head. But the basic glove portion is the same as every other glove with a thumb increase you've made, just like my **Super Simple Fingerless Gloves** only done with a purl stitch, the backside of a stockinette stitches, to make the spider stand out even more.

This pattern has been in the works for a number of years now. It originally started as a knit in the round design, but because of the extensive purling, there were always lines left where the needles met. I couldn't live with that.

So, there was a change in plans from the initial design. First change; it's knit flat on 2 needles. The second is that instead of including a bunch of how-to pictures, and there were going to be a lot, I decided it was time to utilize QR codes. Everything that may be challenging, particularly rows 25 – 27 can be a little confusing. I made videos that show the trickier parts of these rows. To watch the video, take a picture of the QR code with your phone or tablet and the video will pop up. You can watch the video instantly as many times as you need.

If you are reading this on your phone, tablet or computer, you can click the link provided instead. The same video pops up on my website regardless.

A couple words of advice before we get started, this isn't a pattern for beginners. I recommend that you have some basic knowledge of knitting. I also suggest making a pair of my plain fingerless gloves first if you've never made a pair of gloves or mittens before. Thumb gussets can be tricky and there's no point adding in a spider to confuse things even more.

Wrong Stitch Counts

It is very easy to have the wrong number of stitches created around the spider. This can happen between the gusset for the thumb and the spider, or for the shorter side. If that happens you can take it apart. The other option is to just go with it. Being a stitch or two off won't be noticeable to the wearer.

If you decide to "just go for it", line up the stitches done to create the spider to previous spider stitches. In general, this is just the legs. They are very obvious. Keep in mind that you always knit the legs on the right side and purl the legs on the wrong side. Adjust the background of the mitt with your incorrect count of purl stitches on the right side and the knit stitches on the wrong side.

For example, if you're making Row 30, instead of K7 at the start of the row you made a mistake and now have K8. Knit the 8 stitches instead and start the rest of the pattern from there.

Example row:
> **Row 30:** K7 *P1 K1* Repeat from * to * 2 *more* times. P1 K6 M1 K11 M1 K12

Things You Need

Worsted weight yarn – a standard ball of yarn (215 yards/197 m)

Knitting needles – described below in sizing and gauge

Cable Needle

Stitch Holder

Tapestry needle to sew the seam and work in the ends

Gauge

Small

size 3.5 mm (US size 4)
11 stitches every 2 inches (5 cm)
16 rows every 2 inches (5 cm)

Medium

size 4 mm (US size 6)
10 stitches every 2 inches (5 cm)
14 rows every 2 inches (5 cm)

Large

size 5 mm (US size 8)
9 stitches every 2 inches (5 cm)
12 rows every 2 inches (5 cm)

Left Hand

Cast on 33, loosely

Row 1: K1 P1 across. K last st.

Row 2: P1 K1 across. P last st.

Repeat rows 1 and 2 for a total of 10 rows.

Row 11: P across

Row 12: K across

Row 13: P across

Row 14: K across

Row 15: P12 PM1 P1 PM1 P7 K1 P3 K1 P8   (35 sts)

Row 16: K8 P1 K3 P1 K22   (35 sts)

Row 17: P20 K1 P1 K1 P3 K1 P1 K1 P6   (35 sts)

Row 18: K6 P1 K1 P1 K3 P1 K1 P1 K5 M1 K3 M1 K12   (37 sts)

Row 19: P22 K1 P1 K1 P3 K1 P1 K1 P6   (37 sts)

Row 20: K6 P1 K1 P1 K3 P1 K1 P1 K22   (37 sts)

Row 21: P12 PM1 P5 PM1 P5 C1F twice, P1, C1B twice, P6   (39 sts)

Row 22: K6 *K1 P1* Repeat from *to * 3 *more* times, K25   (39 sts)

Row 23: P25 C1F K1 P1 K1 C1B P7   (39 sts)

Row 24: K8 P2 K1 P2 K7 M1 K7 M1 K12   (41 sts)

Row 25: P28 K2tog, Bobble 6 (K6 into one stitch by alternating knitting into the front and back of the stitch, turn. *Working the following rows into the 6 stitches in the one stitch*, P6, turn, K6, turn, P6, turn, K6, turn, P6, turn, K6, turn, P6, turn, K2tog 3 times (do *NOT* turn). Pass the middle stitch over the stitch closest to the tip of the needle. Two bobble stitches remain. Pass the second bobble stitch over the stitch closest to the tip of the needle. (The bobble is now 1 stitch again on your needle.) K2tog. P8   (39 sts)

Take a photo of this QR code to
watch the how-to video for Row 25

Row 26: K8 PM1 P3tog PM1 K28   (39 sts)

Video for Row 26

Row 27: P12 PM1 P9 PM1 P7 FB2 (This is a simple increase knit-wise in the next stitch. These are

the start of the front legs). Bobble 5 (K5 into one stitch by alternating knitting into the front and back of

the stitch, turn. ***Working the following rows into the 5 stitches in the one stitch***, P5, turn, K5, turn,

P2tog P1 P2tog, turn, K3 (do ***NOT*** turn). Pass the middle stitch over the stitch closest to the tip of the

needle. Two bobble stitches remain. Pass the second bobble stitch over the stitch closest to the tip of

the needle. (The bobble is now 1 stitch again on your needle) FB2 (AKA Increase in the next stitch.

Makes the other front legs). P8.   (43 sts)

Video for Row 27

Row 28: K8 P2 K1 P2 K30   (43 sts)

Row 29: P29 C1B K1 P1 K1 C1F P7   (43 sts)

Row 30: K7 *P1 K1* Repeat from * to * 2 *more* times. P1 K6 M1 K11 M1 K12   (45 sts)

Row 31: P30 C1B twice P1 C1F twice P6   (45 sts)

Row 32: K6 P1 K1 P1 K3 P1 K1 P1 K30   (45 sts)

Row 33: P12. Pass the next 13 stitches to a stitch holder. P7 K1 P3 K1 P8   (32 sts)

Row 34: K8 P1 K3 P1 K19   (32 sts)

Row 35: P across

Row 36: K across

Row 37: P across

Row 38: K across

Row 39 - 42: K1 P1 across

Cast off *loosely*.

Making the Thumb

Pick up the 13 stitches on the stitch holder. Transfer them onto the other needle so you start knitting

with the **WRONG** side facing you. If you don't transfer them onto the other needle you'll get a line.

Row 1: K across

Row 2: P across

Row 3: K across

Cast off *loosely*.

Right Hand

Cast on 33, loosely

Row 1: K1 P1 across. K last st.

Row 2: P1 K1 across. P last st.

Repeat rows 1 and 2 for a total of 10 rows.

Row 11: P across

Row 12: K across

Row 13: P across

Row 14: K across

Row 15: P8 K1 P3 K1 P7 PM1 P1 PM1 P12   (35 sts)

Row 16: K22 P1 K3 P1 K8   (35 sts)

Row 17: P6 K1 P1 K1 P3 K1 P1 K1 P20   (35 sts)

Row 18: K12 M1 K3 M1 K5 P1 K1 P1 K3 P1 K1 P1 K6   (37 sts)

Row 19: P6 K1 P1 K1 P3 K1 P1 K1 P22   (37 sts)

Row 20: K22 P1 K1 P1 K3 P1 K1 P1 K6   (37 sts)

Row 21: P6 C1F twice, P1, C1B twice, P5 PM1 P5 PM1 P12   (39 sts)

Row 22: K24 *K1 P1* Repeat from *to * 3 *more* times, K7   (39 sts)

Row 23: P7 C1F K1 P1 K1 C1B P25   (39 sts)

Row 24: K12 M1 K7 M1 K7 P2 K1 P2 K8   (41 sts)

Row 25: P8 K2tog, Bobble 6 (K6 into one stitch by alternating knitting into the front and back of the stitch, turn. ***Working the following rows into the 6 stitches in the one stitch***, P6, turn, K6, turn, P6, turn, K6, turn, K6, turn, P6, turn, K6, turn, P6, turn, K2tog 3 times (do ***NOT*** turn). Pass the middle stitch over the stitch closest to the tip of the needle. Two bobble stitches remain. Pass the second bobble stitch over the stitch closest to the tip of the needle. (The bobble is now 1 stitch again on your needle.) K2tog. P28   (39 sts)

Row 26: K28 PM1 P3tog PM1 K8   (39 sts)

Row 27: P8 FB2 (This is a simple increase knit-wise in the next stitch. These are the start of the front legs). Bobble 5 (K5 into one stitch by alternating knitting into the front and back of the stitch, turn. ***Working the following rows into the 5 stitches in the one stitch***, P5, turn, K5, turn, P2tog P1 P2tog, turn, K3 (do ***NOT*** turn). Pass the middle stitch over the stitch closest to the tip of the needle. Two bobble stitches remain. Pass the second bobble stitch over the stitch closest to the tip of the needle. (There is now 1 stitch on your needle.) FB2 (AKA Increase in the next stitch. Makes the other front legs). P7 PM1 P9 PM1 P12.   (43 sts)

Row 28: K30 P2 K1 P2 K8   (43 sts)

Row 29: P7 C1B K1 P1 K1 C1F P29   (43 sts)

Row 30: K12 M1 K11 M1 K6 P1 *K1 P1* Repeat from * to * 2 ***more*** times. K7   (45 sts)

Row 31: P6 C1B twice P1 C1F twice P30   (45 sts)

Row 32: K30 P1 K1 P1 K3 P1 K1 P1 K6   (45 sts)

Row 33: P8 K1 P3 K1 P7 Pass the next 13 stitches to a stitch holder P12   (32 sts)

Row 34: K19 P1 K3 P1 K8   (32 sts)

Row 35: P across

Row 36: K across

Row 37: P across

Row 38: K across

Row 39 - 42: K1 P1 across

Cast off *loosely*.

Making the Thumb

Pick up the 13 stitches on the stitch holder. Transfer them onto the other needle so you start knitting

with the **WRONG** side facing you. If you don't transfer them onto the other needle you'll get a line.

Row 1: K across

Row 2: P across

Row 3: K across

Cast off *loosely*.

Finishing

I recommend that you finish the body of the spider before sewing the seams along the edge. It's easier to work it when flat. I like to make a figure 8 around the body, to the head, around the head, and back to the start.

To give the spider body and head a more rounded feel, cut a length of yarn about 12" long. Insert your tapestry needle from the wrong side through the front between the head and the body. Pick up stitches around the edge of the body, back to the head. Pull snug until you are happy with the body shape

Pick up stitches around the head back to the body. Pull snug until you're happy with the shape.

Pull the yarn to the back of your work. Tie off.

I like to tack the body at it's base to the glove so it won't flop around and stay in line with the head. Tie off.

No need to work in the ends when finishing the spider body and head. Simply pull the yarn through the body of the spider. Press the body down and cut the yarn. When the body pops back up, the end will be hidden in the body.

Once the spider finishing is complete, sew the seams along the edge and the thumb, working in the ends when finished to avoid lumps from knots.

Abbreviations

K - Knit

P - Purl

st – stitch

sts – stitches

P3tog – Purl 3 stitches together

P2tog – Purl 2 stitches together

K2tog – Knit 2 stitches together

K3tog – Knit 3 stitches together

PM1 – Make one (purl wise). Increase one stitch between the stitches. Pick up the yarn between the stitches. Twist it slightly and place it on your non-working needle. Purl the stitch. Watch this video on **How to PM1 or Purl Make 1** to see how.

M1 – Make one (knit wise). Increase one stitch between the stitches. Pick up the yarn between the stitches. Twist it slightly and place it on your non-working needle. Knit the stitch. Watch this video on **How to M1 or Make 1** to see how.

C1B – Cable 1 back. Pick up next stitch on a cable needle. Pull this stitch to the ***BACK*** of your work. **Knit** the next stitch. **Purl** the stitch on the cable needle. Watch this video on **How to Cable 1 Back** to see how.

C1F – Cable 1 forward. Pick up the next stitch on a cable needle. Pull this stitch to the ***FRONT*** of your work. **Purl** the next stitch. **Knit** the stitch on the cable needle. Watch this video on **How to Cable 1 Forward** to see how.

FB2 – Knit in the front and back of the next stitch. This is also known as an increase one in the next stitch. I'm labeling it as this because it is very easy to make a mistake here and pick up an extra stitch. This way I know I have your attention and made you look ☺ No need to thank me..or complain. Both seem to be a likely response tbh.

QR Codes to All Videos

To make this very simple and to take you over to YouTube directly, here is the playlist of all the videos needed to make these gloves. Take a photo with your phone or tablet to watch them play. Here is the direct link you can type in - **https://bit.ly/spider-sts**

Super Cute
Hippo Fingerless Gloves
Knit Flat with 2 Needles

I originally started this 3D animal adventure with my very popular owl gloves. It then progressed on to my Spider Gloves and Autumn Leaf Gloves. I wanted to make a cat sitting down on a pair of fingerless mitts. Well, that didn't turn out as expected but it is how these hippo gloves came to be. I'm still working on the cat gloves...

When making these, I realized that I couldn't make it in the traditional way by starting at the cuff and working my way to the fingers. I had to go the opposite way to be able to make the arms, legs, body, head and ears. No problem. I rewrote the basic glove pattern. That's the first pattern in this publocation.

Anyways, the pattern is written separately for both the right and left hand. Because it is knit flat there is a seam that runs along the outside of the hand and along the pinky finger. The thumb is knitted once the hand is completed with picked up stitches. And also, the hippo will never fall off. It's made as you make the glove by going back and forth and making formed bobbles. Other than the thumb, this is made in one piece.

I've added photos in the rows of the pattern that have trickier parts like making the bobbles, belly and decreases. If you are a seasoned knitter and don't need the photos, I've written out the rows again without the photos. Regardless...***you only need to knit each row once!***

Things You Need

Worsted weight yarn – 1 standard ball of yarn (215 yards/197 m). Any colours of your choosing.

Knitting needles:

   Small - Size 3 US (3.25 mm) knitting needles

   Medium - Size 6 US (4 mm) knitting needles

   Large - Size 8 US (5 mm) knitting needles

Tapestry needle - to sew the seam and work in the ends.

0.27 inch (7mm) wiggle eyes or small buttons. You can also embroider eyes on if you prefer.

Gauge

In *stockinette* stitch

Small

size 3.5 mm (US size 4) knitting needles
11 stitches every 2 inches (5 cm)
16 rows every 2 inches (5 cm)

Medium

size 4 mm (US size 6) knitting needles
10 stitches every 2 inches (5 cm)
14 rows every 2 inches (5 cm)

Large

size 5 mm (US size 8) knitting needles
9 stitches every 2 inches (5 cm)
12 rows every 2 inches (5 cm)

Right Hand

Cast on 34

Row 1: (P1 K2). Repeat to the last st. P1.

Row 2: (K1 P2) Repeat to the last st. K1.

Repeat these 2 rows for a total of 6 rows. (If you want to change colours, do so now.)

Row 7 – 12: Knit across

Row 13: K14 Cast on 13 sts. K20. (47 sts) Click this link or scan/take a photo of the QR code with your phone or tablet if you need help with casting on.

Row 14: Knit across

Row 15 (Feet): K35 Bobble 3 (K3 into one stitch. by alternating knitting into the front, the back and the front of the stitch, turn. ***Working the following rows into the 3 stitches in the one stitch***, P3, turn, K3, turn, P3, turn, K3tog (do ***NOT*** turn).

3 sts in one st

Turn and purl

Done working the rows

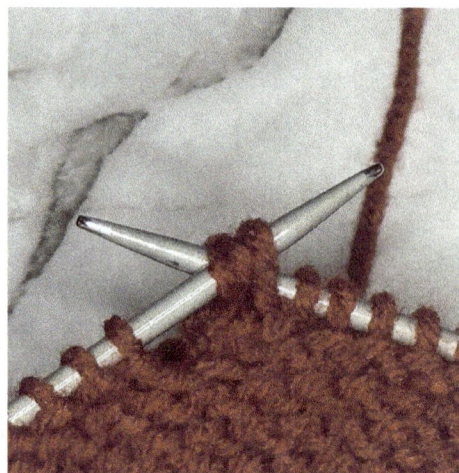

*Knit 3 sts together from **RIGHT** to **LEFT***

Stitch completed

K2,

Next 2 sts knitted and going to make another bobble.

Bobble 3 (as before),

*Knit the 2 sts together in this bobble from **LEFT** to **RIGHT***

2ⁿᵈ bobble done

K8.

Row 15 repeated without the photos

Row 15 (Feet): K35 Bobble 3 (K3 into one stitch. by alternating knitting into the front, the back and the front of the stitch, turn. ***Working the following rows into the 3 stitches in the one stitch***, P3, turn, K3, turn, P3, turn, K3tog (do ***NOT*** turn). K2, Bobble 3 (as before), K8.

Row 16: K8 P4 K35

Row 17 (Belly): K14, K2tog K9, K2tog, K9. (K3 into one stitch) twice. Turn. ***Working the following rows into the 6 stitches in the two stitches***,

6 sts in 2 sts

P6, turn, K1, *M1* K4 *M1*, K1 turn,

Increased to 8 sts

P8, turn, K8, turn, P8, turn, K8 (do **NOT** turn.

Repeated rows for bottom of the belly done.

Continue to work the remaining stitches of the row) *K9. (51 sts)*

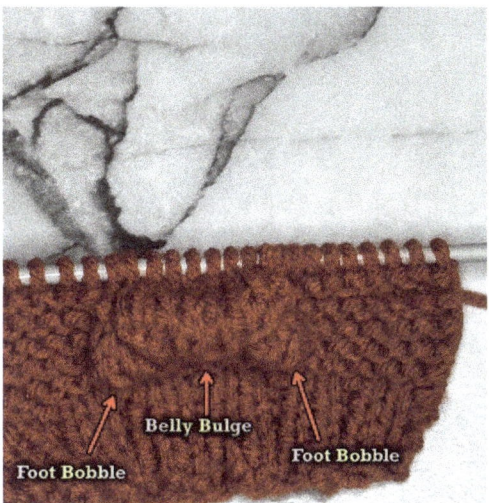

Row 17 completed (for left hand)

Row 17 repeated without the photos

Row 17 (Belly): K14, K2tog K9, K2tog, K9. (K3 into one stitch) twice. Turn. ***Working the following rows into the 6 stitches in the two stitches***, P6, turn, K1, *M1* K4 *M1*, K1 turn, P8, turn, K8, turn, P8, turn, K8 (do **NOT** turn. Continue to work the remaining stitches of the row) K9. (51 sts)

Row 18: K9 P8 K34

Row 19: K across

Row 20: K9 P8 K34

Row 21: K14, K2tog K7 K2tog, K9, K2tog (When making this stitch, pick up a stitch as if to knit. Twist the stitch and place it back on your non-working needle. Knit the 2 stitches together from right to left.)

Insert your needle as if to knit

Place the loop on your working needle and twist

Place the st back on your non-working needle

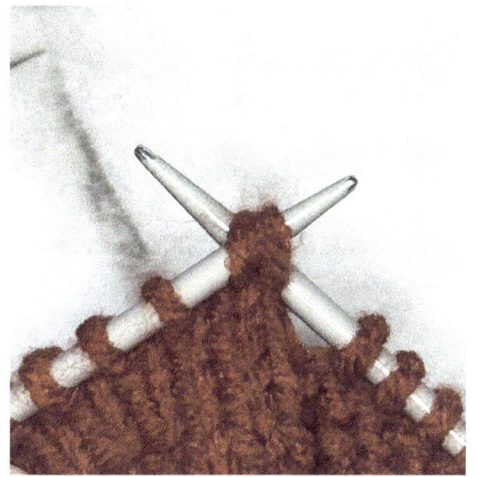

*Knit the 2 sts together from **RIGHT** to **LEFT**.*

There is a video I made for another pattern that shows
how to twist the stitch to get the nice edge.
Scan the QR code or click this link:
<u>How to K2tog for Leaf Motif Edges</u>

K4 K2tog (knit the stitches together from left to right as you normally would.), K9. (47 sts)

Row 21 repeated without the photos

Row 21: K14, K2tog K7 K2tog, K9, K2tog (When making this stitch, pick up a stitch as if to knit.

Twist the stitch and place it back on your non-working needle. Knit the 2 stitches together from right to

left.) K4 K2tog (knit the stitches together from left to right as you normally would.), K9. (47 sts)

Row 22: K9 P6 K32

Row 23 (Arms): K31 Bobble 3, K2tog (like you did before: pick up, twist, knit right to left) K2, K2tog

(knit the stitches together from left to right.), Bobble 3, K8. (45 sts)

Row 24: K9, P4 K32

Row 25 (Neck): K14, K2tog K5 K2tog, K9, K2tog (like you did before: pick up, twist, knit right to

left), K2tog (knit the stitches together from left to right.) K9. (41 sts)

Row 26: K9 P2 K30

Row 27 (Head): K30 (K3 into one stitch) twice. Turn. ***Working the following rows into the 6 stitches in the two stitches***, P6, turn, K1, M1 K4 M1, K1 turn, P8, turn, K8, turn, P8, turn, K8, turn, P8, turn, K8 (do **NOT** turn. Continue to work the remaining stitches of the row), K9. (47 sts)

Row 28: K9 P8 K30

Row 29: K14, K2tog K3 K2tog, K9, K2tog (like you did before: pick up, twist, knit right to left) K4 K2tog (knit the stitches together from left to right.), K9. (43 sts)

Row 30: K9 P6 K28

Row 31 (Ears): K28 K2tog (as you did before) AND make a Bobble 3 (pick up 3 sts by knitting into the front, back and front of the 2 sts you're knitting together).

Flip the st and K2tog from **RIGHT** to **LEFT...**

...and make 3 sts in the K2tog.
Continue to make a Bobble 3 like before.

K2, K2tog AND make Bobble 3,

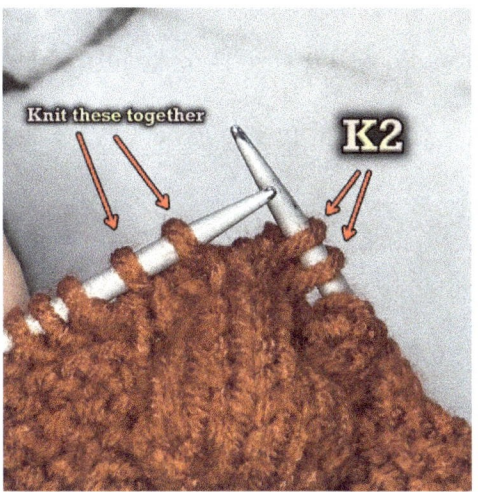

*Knit the 2 sts together from **LEFT** to **RIGHT**...*

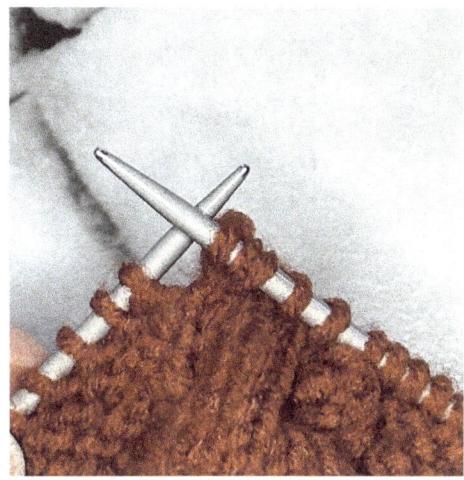

...and start the bobble 3 (3 sts in K2tog)

K9. (41 sts)

Row 31 repeated without the photos

Row 31 (Ears): K28 K2tog (as you did before) AND make a Bobble 3 (pick up 3 sts by knitting into the front, back and front of the 2 sts you're knitting together). K2, K2tog AND make Bobble 3, K9. (41 sts)

Row 32: K across

Row 33: K14, K2tog K1 K2tog, K8, K2tog, K2 K2tog, K8 (37 sts)

♥ **Row 34 – 38:** Knit across

With the **RIGHT** side facing (If you want to change colours, do so now.)

*__Row 39:__ (P1 K2). Repeat to the last st. P1.

Row 40: (K1 P2) Repeat to the last st. K1.*

Repeat from * to * for a total of 12 rows.

Cast off. Be sure to follow the P1 K2 pattern to create a nice, finished edge.

Make the Thumb

With the **RIGHT** side facing, Pick up 13 sts from the additional sts you cast on in Row 13. Pick up the st in the twist formed from casting on. If you need help you can scan the following QR code or click this link – Pick up Thumb Stitches.

With the **WRONG** side facing

Row 1: (K1 P2) Repeat to the last st. K1.

Row 2: (P1 K2) Repeat to the last st. P1.

Row 3: Repeat row 1

Cast off following maintaining the P1 K2 pattern.

Sew the seams on the thumb and side of the glove.

Left Hand

Cast on 34

Row 1: (P1 K2). Repeat to the last st. P1.

Row 2: (K1 P2) Repeat to the last st. K1.

Repeat these 2 rows for a total of 6 rows. (If you want to change colours, do so now.)

Row 7 – 12: Knit across

Row 13: K20 Cast on 13 sts. K14. (47 sts)

Row 14: Knit across

Row 15 (Feet): K8 Bobble 3 (K3 into one stitch. by alternating knitting into the front, the back and the front of the stitch, turn. *Working the following rows into the 3 stitches in the one stitch*, P3, turn, K3, turn, P3, turn, K3tog (do *NOT* turn). K2, Bobble 3 (as before), K35.

Row 16: K35 P4 K8

Row 17 (Belly): K9, (K3 into one stitch) twice. Turn. *Working the following rows into the 6 stitches in the two stitches*, P6, turn, K1, M1 K4 M1, K1 turn, P8, turn, K8, turn, P8, turn, K8 (do **NOT** turn. Continue to work the remaining stitches of the row) K9, K2tog K9, K2tog. K14. (51 sts)

Row 18: K34 P8 K9

Row 19: K across

Row 20: K34 P8 K9

Row 21: K9, K2tog (When making this stitch, pick up a stitch as if to knit. Twist the stitch and place it back on your non-working needle. Knit the 2 stitches together from right to left.) K4 K2tog (knit the stitches together from left to right.), K9 K2tog K7 K2tog, K14. (47 sts)

Row 22: K32 P6 K9

Row 23 (Arms): K8 Bobble 3, K2tog (like you did before: pick up, twist, knit right to left) K2, K2tog (knit the stitches together from left to right.), Bobble 3, K31. (45 sts)

Row 24: K32, P4 K9

Row 25 (Neck): K9, K2tog (like you did before: pick up, twist, knit right to left), K2tog (knit the stitches together from left to right.) K9, K2tog K5 K2tog, K14. (41 sts)

Row 26: K30 P2 K9

Row 27 (Head): K9 (K3 into one stitch) twice. Turn. ***Working the following rows into the 6 stitches in the two stitches***, P6, turn, K1, M1 K4 M1, K1 turn, P8, turn, K8, turn, P8, turn, K8, turn, P8, turn, K8 (do **NOT** turn. Continue to work the remaining stitches of the row), K30. (47 sts)

Row 28: K30 P8 K9

Row 29: K9, K2tog (like you did before: pick up, twist, knit right to left) K4 K2tog (knit the stitches together from left to right.), K9, K2tog K3 K2tog, K14. (43 sts)

Row 30: K28 P6 K9

Row 31 (Ears): K9 K2tog AND make a Bobble 3 (pick up 3 sts by knitting into the front, back and front of the 2 sts you're knitting together). K2, K2tog AND make Bobble 3, K28. (41 sts)

Row 32: K across

Row 33: K8, K2tog, K2 K2tog, K8, K2tog K1 K2tog K14. (37 sts)

♥ **Row 34 – 38:** Knit across

With the **RIGHT** side facing (If you want to change colours, do so now.)

***Row 39:** (P1 K2). Repeat to the last st. P1.

Row 40: (K1 P2) Repeat to the last st. K1.*

Repeat from * to * for a total of 12 rows.

Cast off. Be sure to follow the P1 K2 pattern to create a nice, finished edge.

Make the Thumb

With the **RIGHT** side facing, Pick up 13 sts from the additional sts you cast on in Row 13. Pick up the st in the twist formed from casting on. If you need help you can scan the following QR code or click this link – Pick up Thumb Stitches.

With the **WRONG** side facing

Row 1: (K1 P2) Repeat to the last st. K1.

Row 2: (P1 K2) Repeat to the last st. P1.

Row 3: Repeat row 1

Cast off following maintaining the P1 K2 pattern.

Sew the seams on the thumb and side of the glove.

Hints and Tips

While not necessary, I like to pull the arms closer together for a thinner neck and more noticeable belly. From the back, pass your needle to the front. Pass the yarn over the noticeable decrease stitch beside the arm and under the chest. Go up on the other side of the chest, catch the decrease stitch and pass through the hole next to the arm. Pull together as tight as you like. I leave a bit of slackness.

Catch the sts on the sides like this.
Use the same colour as your hippo.
I used a contrasting colour to showcase the sts.

Pull the yarn snug.

Tie off and work in the ends.

If you would like a longer glove, make more rows than indicated with the row marked with the ♥ If you are making a longer glove, cast the stitches off loosely to allow for more stretch.

If you want the cuff to be a different colour than the rest of the glove, I've indicated when to switch colours. The cuff on the fingers, wrist and thumb are done with the K1 P2 ribbing sections.

You don't need to add the extra ribbing for the thumb. It is a finished edge so it won't come undone. You may want to do a quick single crochet around to give it a bit of a fancy edging.

Watch the Helpful Video

If you need help with casting on the thumb or picking up the stitches to finish the thumb, you can watch the quick how-to video on Youtube here - <u>Basic Fingerless Gloves - How to Make the Thumb</u>

You can also take a pic of the QR code below. When you take a photo, a link will pop up on your phone or tablet. Tap the link and the video will automatically start to play.

Abbreviations

k - knit

p - purl

k2tog - knit 2 sts together

K3tog – knit 3 sts together

st - stitch

sts - stitches

M1 – Make one (knit wise). Increase one stitch between the stitches. Pick up the yarn between the stitches. Twist slightly. Place it on your non-working needle. Knit the stitch. Watch this video to see how.

Lattice
Fingerless Gloves

Before we dive in, I want to give you a heads-up: this pattern isn't for beginners. But don't worry, I've included some photos to guide you along the way. I'm assuming you're already familiar with carrying yarn behind your work to change colours. It's not too tricky, but do keep an eye on your tension—consistency is key!

I'm really happy with how this pattern turned out! It took a bit of trial and error to incorporate the lattice design into the gloves, but now that I've nailed it, I'm already dreaming up other projects to use it in. (Hint: slippers might be next! ☺)

Things You Need

Worsted weight yarn – 1 standard ball of yarn (215 yards/197 m) will make the gloves in one colour. Any colour combinations of your choosing will work.

Knitting needles:

  Small - Size 6 US (4 mm) knitting needles

  Medium - Size 8 US (5 mm) knitting needles

  Large - Size 10 US (6 mm) knitting needles

Cable Needle

Tapestry needle - to sew the seam and work in the ends.

Gauge

In *stockinette* stitch

Small

size 4 mm (US size 6) knitting needles
10 stitches every 2 inches (5 cm)
14 rows every 2 inches (5 cm)

Medium

size 5 mm (US size 8) knitting needles
9 stitches every 2 inches (5 cm)
12 rows every 2 inches (5 cm)

Large

size 6 mm (US size 10) knitting needles
8 stitches every 2 inches (5 cm)
10 rows every 2 inches (5 cm)

Colours

MC – Main colour. The colour of the cuffs and lattice design

BG – Background colour. The colour the lattice is on. The palm and back of the hand.

HC – Highlight colour. The band at the end of the wrist section and start of the cuff at the fingers

Continue using the colour until stated to change in the pattern.

You can use more colours than the 3 colours listed. You can use one colour and made tone on tone fingerless mitts. It's up to you.

Right Hand

Cast on 33 sts

Row 1: With MC K across

Row 2: P across. Repeat row 1 and 2 for a total of 8 rows.

Row 9: K across

Row 10: *K1 P2* Repeat from * to * to the end of the row. Repeat rows 9 and 10 for a total of 10 rows. Carry yarn behind your work for row 23 (saves an end to work in)

Row 19: With HC K5 *M1 K6* Repeat from * to * 3 times more. M1 K4 (38 sts This count is constant until you start making the thumb gusset. Stitch counts are given for the increases.)

Row 20 – 22: K across. Break yarn at the end of row 22.

Row 23: *With MC K. With BG K5* Repeat from * to * 3 times more. With MC K. With BG K13. Break BG colour.

Row 24: Pass next 13 sts onto working needle. With MC YF, Sl st as if to purl. *YB Sl 5sts as if to purl, YF Sl st as if to purl,* repeat to the end of the row. (Don't work this stitch. Let yarn hang).

Row 25: Join BG K across.

Row 26: P across.

☼ ♣ **Row 27:** With MC K1. Keep YB for this row. Sl 2sts as if to purl *LK, Sl 5sts as if to purl* Repeat from * to * 2 more times more. LK, Sl 2sts purl-wise K next st. Leave remaining sts unworked. Turn. (see *Abbreviations* for photos to LK).

♦ **Row 28:** With MC YF Sl st. YB Sl 2sts purl-wise *YF Sl st purl-wise, YB Sl 5sts purl-wise* Repeat from * to * 2 times more. YF Sl st purl-wise YB Sl 2sts purl-wise YF Sl st purl-wise

Row 29: With BG K across

Row 30: P across

♥ **Row 31:** With MC *LK, Sl 5sts purl-wise* Repeat from * to * 3 times more. LK. Leave remaining sts unworked. Turn.

■ **Row 32:** With MC Sl st purl-wise * YB Sl 5sts purl-wise, YF Sl st purl-wise, * Repeat from * to * 3 times more.

Row 33: With BG K across

Row 34: P across ☼ Repeat from ☼ to ☼ one more time. If you would like a longer length between the cuff and wrist, do more repeats.

Row 35: Repeat ♣ Row 27

Row 36: Repeat ♦ Row 28

Row 37: With BG K26 M1 K M1 K11 (40 sts)

Row 38: P across

Row 39: Repeat ♥ Row 31

Row 40: Repeat ■ Row 32

Row 41: With BG K across

Row 42: P12 PM1 P PM1 P27 (42 sts)

Row 43: Repeat ♣ Row 27

Row 44: Repeat ♦ Row 28

Row 45: With BG K across

Row 46: P across

Row 47: Repeat ♥ Row 31

Row 48: Repeat ■ Row 32

Row 49: With BG K28 M1 K M1 K13 (44 sts)

Row 50: P across

Row 51: Repeat ♣ Row 27

Row 52: Repeat ♦ Row 28

Row 53: With BG K across

Row 54: P14 PM1 P1 PM1 P29 (46 sts)

Row 55: Repeat ♥ Row 31

Row 56: Repeat ■ Row 32

Row 57: With BG K across

Row 58: P across

Row 59: Repeat ♣ Row 27

Row 60: Repeat ♦ Row 28

Row 61: With BG K30 M1 K1 M1 K15 (48 sts)

Row 62: P across

Row 63: Repeat ♥ Row 31

Row 64: Repeat ■ Row 32

Row 65: With BG K across

Row 66: P16 PM1 P PM1 P31 (50 sts)

Row 67: Repeat ♣ Row 27

Row 68: Repeat ♦ Row 28

Row 69: With BG K across

Row 70: P across

Row 71: Repeat ♥ Row 31

Row 72: Repeat ■ Row 32

Row 73: With BG K26 Pass next 13 sts onto a stitch holder. K11 (37 sts)

Row 74: P across. Break BG yarn

Row 75: Repeat ♣ Row 27. Break MC yarn. Pass the 25 sts just worked onto the other needle with 12 unworked stitches.

Row 76: With HC K4 * K2tog K7* Repeat from * to * 2 times more.K2tog K4 (33 sts)

Row 77-79: Knit across

Row 80: With MC K across

Row 81: *K P2* Repeat from * to * to the end of the row.

Row 82: Repeat row 80

Row 83: Repeat row 81

Cast off.

Make Thumb

Transfer the 13 stitches on the stitch holder, back onto your knitting needle.

☺ **Row 1:** With MC K across

♪ **Row 2:** *K P2* Repeat from * to * to the last st. K

Row 3: Repeat ☺ Row 1

Row 4: Repeat ♪ Row 2

Cast off

Sew seams along the thumb and the side of the gloves.

Left Hand

Cast on 33 sts

Row 1: With MC K across

Row 2: P across. Repeat row 1 and 2 for a total of 8 rows.

Row 9: K across

Row 10: *K1 P2* Repeat from * to * to the end of the row. Repeat rows 9 and 10 for a total of 10 rows. Break yarn.

Row 19: With HC K5 *M1 K6* Repeat from * to * 3 times more. M1 K4 (38 sts. This count is constant until you start making the thumb gusset. Stitch counts are given for the increases.)

Row 20 – 22: K across. Break yarn at end of row 22.

Row 23: With BG K13.*With MC K. With BG K5* Repeat from * to * 3 times more. With MC K. Break BG colour.

Row 24: With MC and YF Sl st as if to purl. *YB Sl 5sts as if to purl, YF Sl st as if to purl,* repeat from * to * 3 times more. YF. Pass next 13 sts onto working needle.

Row 25: Join BG K across.

Row 26: P across

⊙ **§ Row 27:** With BG K13. With MC cross yarn under BG yarn then K1. Keep YB for this row. Sl 2sts as if to purl *LK, Sl 5sts as if to purl* Repeat from * to * 2 more times. LK, Sl 2sts purl-wise K next st. (see *Hints and Tips* and *Abbreviations* for photos to cross yarn and LK respectively).

⌂ **Row 28:** With MC YF Sl st. YB Sl 2sts purl-wise * YF Sl st purl-wise, YB Sl 5sts purl-wise* Repeat from * to * 2 times more. YF Sl st purl-wise YB Sl 2sts purl-wise YF Sl st purl-wise . Leave remaining sts unworked. Turn.

◊ **Row 29:** With BG K25 over the 25 sts from previous row.

Row 30: P across.

Ө **Row 31:** With BG K13 With MC cross yarn under BG yarn then *LK, Sl 5sts purl-wise* Repeat from * to * 3 times more. LK. (40 sts)

▲ **Row 32:** With MC Sl st purl-wise *YB Sl 5sts purl-wise, YF Sl st purl-wise* Repeat from * to * 3 times more. Turn. Leave remaining sts unworked.

Row 33: Repeat ◊ row 29

Row 34: P across. ⊙ Repeat from ⊙ to ⊙ one more time. If you would like a longer length between the cuff and wrist, do more repeats.

Row 35: With BG K11 M1 K M1 K1 With MC cross yarn under BG yarn then K1 Keep YB for this row. Sl 2sts as if to purl *LK, Sl 5sts as if to purl* Repeat from * to * 2 more times. LK, Sl 2sts purl-wise K next st. (40 sts)

Row 36: Repeat ⌂ Row 28.

Row 37: Repeat ◊ row 29

Row 38: P across

Row 39: With BG K15 With MC cross yarn under BG yarn then *LK, Sl 5sts purl-wise* Repeat from * to * 3 times more. LK.

Row 40: Repeat ▲ Row 32

Row 41: Repeat ◊ row 29

Row 42: P27 PM1 P PM1 P12. (42 sts)

Row 43: With BG K17. With MC cross yarn under BG yarn then K1. Keep YB for this row. Sl 2sts as if to purl *LK, Sl 5sts as if to purl* Repeat from * to * 2 more times. LK, Sl 2sts purl-wise K next st.

Row 44: With MC YF Sl st. YB Sl 2sts purl-wise * YF Sl st purl-wise, YB Sl 5sts purl-wise* Repeat from * to * 2 times more. YF Sl st purl-wise YB Sl 2sts purl-wise YF Sl st purl-wise. Leave remaining sts unworked. Turn.

Row 45: Repeat ◊ row 29

Row 46: P across

Row 47: With BG K13 M1 K M1 K3 With MC cross yarn under BG yarn then *LK, Sl 5sts purl-wise* Repeat from * to * 3 times more. LK. (44 sts)

Row 48: Repeat ▲ row 32

Row 49: Repeat ◊ row 29

Row 50: P across

Row 51: With BG K19. With MC cross yarn under BG yarn then K1. Keep YB for this row. Sl 2sts as if to purl *LK, Sl 5sts as if to purl* Repeat from * to * 2 more times. LK, Sl 2sts purl-wise K next st.

Row 52: Repeat ⛫ Row 28

Row 53: Repeat ◊ row 29

Row 54: P29 PM1 P PM1 P14 (46 sts)

Row 55: With BG K21 With MC cross yarn under BG yarn then *LK, Sl 5sts purl-wise* Repeat from * to * 3 times more. LK.

Row 56: Repeat ▲ row 32

Row 57: Repeat ◊ row 29

Row 58: P across.

Row 59: With BG K15 M1 K M1 K5. With MC cross yarn under BG yarn then K1. Keep YB for this row. Sl 2sts as if to purl *LK, Sl 5sts as if to purl* Repeat from * to * 2 more times. LK, Sl 2sts purl-wise K next st. (48 sts)

Row 60: Repeat ⛫ Row 28

Row 61: Repeat ◊ row 29

Row 62: P across

Row 63: With BG K23 With MC cross yarn under BG yarn then *LK, Sl 5sts purl-wise* Repeat from * to * 3 times more. LK.

Row 64: Repeat ▲ Row 32

Row 65: Repeat ◊ row 29

Row 66: P31 PM1 P PM1 P16 (50 sts)

Row 67: With BG K25. With MC cross yarn under BG yarn then K1. Keep YB for this row. Sl 2sts as if to purl *LK, Sl 5sts as if to purl* Repeat from * to * 2 more times. LK, Sl 2sts purl-wise K next st.

Row 68: Repeat ⛫ row 28

Row 69: Repeat ◊ row 29

Row 70: P across

Row 71: With BG K11. Pass the next 13 sts onto a st holder K1 With MC cross yarn under BG yarn then *LK, Sl 5sts as if to purl* Repeat from * to * 3 more times. LK. (37 sts)

Row 72: Repeat ▲ Row 32

Row 73: Repeat ◊ row 29

Row 74: P across

Row 75: With BG K12 Break BG colour yarn. With MC cross yarn under BG yarn then K1. Keep YB for this row. Sl 2sts as if to purl *LK, Sl 5sts as if to purl* Repeat from * to * 2 more times. LK, Sl 2sts purl-wise K next st. Break MC. Pass ALL of the sts just worked onto the non-working needle.

Where the needle point is when done the row.

Where the needle point needs to be at the start of the row

Row 76: With HC K4 *K2tog K7* Repeat from * to * 2 times more. K2tog. K4 (33 sts)

Row 77-79: Knit across. Break yarn.

Row 80: With MC K across

Row 81: *K P2* Repeat from * to * to the last st. K

Row 82: Repeat row 80

Row 83: Repeat row 81

Cast off.

Make Thumb

transfer the 13 stitches on the stitch holder, back onto your knitting needle.

☺ **Row 1:** With MC K to the last st. K

♪ **Row 2:** *K P2* Repeat from * to * to the end of the row.

Row 3: Repeat ☺ Row 1

Row 4: Repeat ♪ Row 2

Cast off

Sew seams along the thumb and the side of the gloves.

Hints and Tips

Don't pull your yarn tight when pulling the yarn across the back of your work. Give enough slack to let the stitches stretch as they should and NOT bunch up. Not doing so will make the gauge significantly smaller and the glove won't fit.

The lattice pattern is worked when the WRONG side is facing you.

The palm of the hand is plain. FYI I tried to make the lattice pattern all over the mitt. It looked and felt weird and had NO stretch.

You don't need to add the rolled edge. Rows 1-8 create the roll. You can start with the ribbing at Row 9.

If you want to have a longer version of the glove than what is written, you may need to add more sts to the 13 st section so it will fit around the forearm. There isn't a lot of stretch to allow for the wide part of the upper forearm.

Crossing over the yarn is straight forward. It needs to look like this or you will get odd shaped stitches.

If you are a left handed knitter, the crossing over of the yarn may need to be done on the right hand instead of the left. I'm not left handed, but logic would dictate things are reversed. In light of you being left handed, I'm assuming this isn't the first time you've run across this issue.

Abbreviations

K – knit

P – Purl

M1 – Make one (knit wise). Increase one stitch between the stitches. Pick up the yarn between the stitches. Twist slightly. Place it on your non-working needle. Knit the stitch. Click this link to watch this video to see how. **How to Make One or M1 – Increase between stitches** or take a pic of the QR code below with your phone or tablet. Tap the link that pops up.

YF – pull the yarn to the **FRONT** of your work

YB – pull the yarn to the **BACK** of your work

Sl st – slip the stitch onto your working needle without working the stitch.

LK – loop knit. Pick up the loop running across between the sts. Knit this and the next st on the needle.

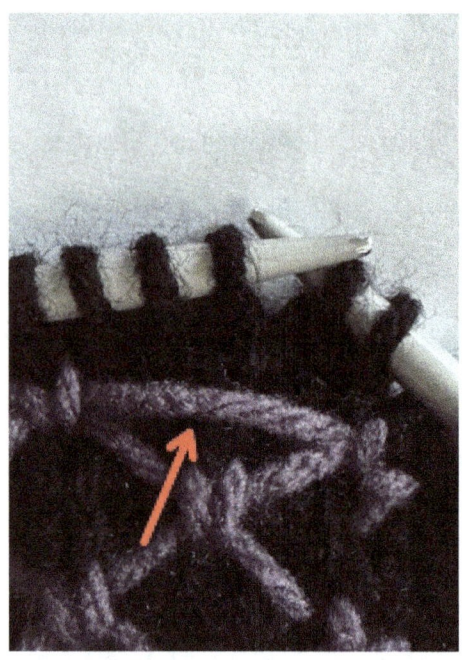

The loop running between sts

Pick up the loop

Knit the next st.

*Knit the st and loop and drop the st from
the non-working needle as you normally would.*

The loops on the edge are slightly harder to see but done the same way.

Yarn is crossed.

Loop between the edge and the st picked up.

Knitting the loop and next st nearly finished.

The loop between the st and the edge is a little harder to see.

Pick up the loop...

...and the last st on the non-working needle.

Work this as you did the others.

PM1 - Make one (purl wise). Increase one stitch between the stitches. Pick up the yarn between the stitches. Twist it slightly and place it on your non-working needle. Purl the stitch. Watch this video on **How to PM1 or Purl Make 1** to see how.

K2tog – knit 2 stitches together.

Like all of my patterns you have my permission to sell and/or give away the physical items that you make using this pattern. You are NOT permitted to reprint this pattern in any form unless you have obtained my written permission to do so.

If you have any questions, please feel free to leave a comment or send me your questions at kweenbee_crafts@hotmail.ca.

Help Support My Work!

Follow me on Instagram, Facebook, Pinterest and YouTube. Every follow, subscribe, thumbs up, like, heart and share help increase my popularity on the web and get more viewers to my work. It costs you nothing but helps me sooooo much!

If you would like to help a little more, you can always become a Website Member to download and print over 50 patterns. Or you can support me by becoming a Patron on Patreon or you can make a single time donation at Buy Me a Coffee.

You can use any of these QR codes to find out more.

Website Member   **Patreon**   **Buy Me a Coffee**

More FREE knitting patterns on my website

I'm always creating new patterns and I post every one of them over on my website. It is an ever growing list so you might want to check out my page at **KweenBee.com**. I design new patterns as I get time. I aim to add a couple new ones each month so the list is always growing!

Below is a VERY small example of the other patterns that I have on the website.

Texting Mittens   Cozy Lace Up Slippers for Adults   Owl Bucket Hat   Winter Beanie Toque or Touque or Tuque with Vertical Stripes

Ultra Thick Slip-On Bootie Slippers   How to Knit a Beanie Hat – with OWLS!   Minimalist Round Toe Slippers   How to Knit a Pair of Flip Mittens or Fingerless Gloves

Of course, none of the links will work. To make it even easier, you can take a photo of the QR code below with your phone or tablet. A link will pop up. Tap that link and it will take you right to the webpage to see all of the patterns including those above.

You can also do a search for the titles online if QR codes are something that you feel you are unable or don't want to use it.

When you are on your favourite search engine like Google, Bing, Yahoo, etc. Enter the term **Kweenbee** and the title as it is written below (capitalization isn't important). It will pop up for you in the search results and be super-easy to find.

For example, enter it like this:

Your results will have my pattern at the very top...usually. Depending on the popularity of the pattern, you may get a link to Pinterest or Ravelry first. Don't worry! All of those options have links back to my original patterns, too!

Follow Me on Social Media

Take a photo with your phone or tablet of the QR codes below. A link will appear. Click the link to go straight to my social media page.